Gay Marriage

Other books in the At Issue series:

Gay Marriage

Kate Burns, *Book Editor*

Bruce Glassman, *Vice President*
Bonnie Szumski, *Publisher*
Helen Cothran, *Managing Editor*

GREENHAVEN PRESS
An imprint of Thomson Gale, a part of The Thomson Corporation

DISCARDED
BRADFORD WG
PUBLIC LIBRARY

Detroit • New York • San Francisco • San Diego • New Haven, Conn.
Waterville, Maine • London • Munich

BRADFORD WG LIBRARY
100 HOLLAND COURT, BOX 130
BRADFORD, ONT. L3Z 2A7

© 2005 Thomson Gale, a part of The Thomson Corporation.

Thomson and Star Logo are trademarks and Gale and Greenhaven Press are registered trademarks used herein under license.

For more information, contact
Greenhaven Press
27500 Drake Rd.
Farmington Hills, MI 48331-3535
Or you can visit our Internet site at http://www.gale.com

LIBRARY OF CONGRESS CATALOGING-IN-PUBLICATION DATA

Gay marriage / Kate Burns, book editor.
   p. cm. — (At issue)
  Includes bibliographical references and index.
  ISBN 0-7377-2376-9 (lib. : alk. paper) — ISBN 0-7377-2377-7 (pbk. : alk. paper)
    1. Same-sex marriage. 2. Same-sex marriage—Religious aspects. 3. Same-sex marriage—Law and legislation. 4. Gay parents—Family relationships. I. Burns, Kate, 1969– . II. At issue (San Diego, Calif.)
  HQ1033.G385 2005
  306.84'8'0973—dc22   2004047445

Printed in the United States of America

Contents

Introduction

On February 24, 2004, President George W. Bush addressed the United States to discuss what he referred to as a matter of "national importance." In an address from the White House he declared:

> The union of a man and woman is the most enduring human institution, honored and encouraged in all cultures and by every religious faith. Ages of experience have taught humanity that the commitment of a husband and wife to love and to serve one another promotes the welfare of children and the stability of society. Marriage cannot be severed from its cultural, religious and natural roots without weakening the good influence of society.

To protect a traditional definition of marriage, he called on Congress to pass an amendment to the U.S. Constitution that would restrict marriage exclusively to opposite-sex couples. As Bush stated, if "the most fundamental institution of civilization" were to include gay couples, the meaning of marriage would change forever with "serious consequences throughout the country."

Prominent supporters and opponents of a federal marriage amendment immediately reacted to the president's proclamation. Gary Bauer, a former Republican presidential candidate, stated, "Every culture in the world, every civilization in the world for over 3,000 years, has defined marriage as the union of one man and one woman. The constitutional amendment merely states that again." On the other side of the fence, National Gay and Lesbian Task Force executive director Matt Foreman characterized support for the amendment as "anti-gay, partisan, divisive and distinctly un-American." Gays and lesbians were not alone in their opposition. San Francisco mayor Gavin Newsom, for example, criticized the president's amendment proposal as "enshrining discrimination in the Constitution." The fervent debate inspired the *San Francisco Chronicle* to call gay marriage "the most divisive civil rights issue in a generation."

The battle to legalize gay marriage

In the 1990s the issue of gay marriage seized the nation's interest when three same-sex couples filed a lawsuit against the state of Hawaii for denying them marriage licenses. Similar claims against gay marriage prohibitions had been filed before in other states, but none had been successful. The Hawaii *Baehr v. Milke* case won on appeal in 1996, and the first court in America declared that banning same-sex couples from marriage is not constitutional. However, before the decision went into effect, popular opposition swelled and voters amended Hawaii's constitution to restrict marriage to heterosexual couples in 1998.

In addition to sparking antagonism within the state of Hawaii, *Baehr v. Milke* generated opposition to gay marriage on a national level. In September 1996 President Bill Clinton signed into law the Defense of Marriage Act (DOMA), which defines marriage for all federal purposes, such as federal laws and taxes, as "a legal union of one man and one woman." DOMA also allows any state to refuse to recognize same-sex unions formalized in other states. Gay marriage opponents, not satisfied with federal measures like DOMA, are working to prevent gay marriages from gaining legal recognition within states and cities as well. To this end, they have introduced legislation to prevent gay couples from filing joint state tax returns and from receiving other state and local marriage benefits in various cities, counties, and states from Washington to Alabama.

Current developments

In recent years advocates and opponents of gay marriage have continued their battle over the issue of gay marriage. Canada made an unprecedented move when its justice panel declared that excluding gays and lesbians from marriage is discrimination. The Canadian court mandated that the federal government align its marriage laws with Canada's Charter of Rights and Freedoms, which legalized gay marriage as of July 2004.

In the United States two state supreme courts have taken similar steps toward legalizing gay marriage. In 1999 Vermont justices ruled that same-sex couples are entitled to all of the protections and benefits that married heterosexual couples receive. The Massachusetts Supreme Court reached the same conclusion in 2003. However, the two states came up with distinctly different solutions to execute the verdict. Vermont created "separate-but-equal" civil unions for same-sex couples but did not give gays and lesbians access to marriage licenses. The Massachusetts court, on the other hand, ruled that same-sex couples be allowed to marry. By committing to issue same-sex couples official marriage licenses, Massachusetts granted gay couples more legal and cultural legitimacy than anywhere in the United States. Same-sex couples in Massachusetts now have the right to a full civil marriage and its hundreds of legal benefits and obligations. The ruling went into effect on May 17, 2004.

On the other side of the country, San Francisco mayor Gavin Newsom joined the movement to legalize gay marriage by ordering the city clerk to issue marriage licenses to same-sex couples on February 12, 2004. Couples lined up by the hundreds and within just three days, more than sixteen hundred same-sex partners were wed. Newsom argued that even though California voters approved a referendum in 2000 defining marriage as the union between a man and a woman, the equal-protection clause of the state constitution trumps the state law and gives gay couples the same right to marry as heterosexuals. A month later California governor Arnold Schwarzenegger ordered the state's attorney general to halt the marriages after more than four thousand couples had wed. Whether the San Francisco gay marriages will be considered valid in the future has yet to be determined.

Gay marriage and the government

The controversy over gay marriage has inspired a great deal of debate about how much power the government should have in marriage issues in a representative democracy. The discussion tends to focus on three main areas: First, people debate the purpose and responsibility of the judiciary in a governmental system that relies on the "checks and balances" of power shared among the executive, legislative, and judicial branches of government. Many arguments focus on whether judges or legislators should have the authority to define marriage. The second debate concerns the balance of power between federal and state interests. Some believe that the federal government should impose uniform marriage laws across the nation. Others argue that states should be able to determine their own laws to regulate marriage within their boundaries. Finally, the third debate is over the historic separation of church and state. Since marriage can be viewed as both a religious institution and a civil procedure, people disagree about whether religious organizations or the government should be entitled to delimit and regulate marriage.

Debates about the role of the government in the United States have challenged citizens since the federal union was formed. Arguments over gay marriage can become passionate because the issue intersects with fundamental questions about the power of government in a democracy.

Guardians of the law or "activist" judges?

The role of the judicial branch of government is delineated in Article III of the U.S. Constitution: "The judicial Power shall extend to all Cases, in Law and Equity, arising under this Constitution, the Laws of the United States, and Treaties made, or which shall be made, under their Authority." The language is broad enough to allow more than one understanding of judicial responsibility. Most Americans agree that judges should interpret laws and ensure their enforcement. Some believe that in interpreting laws, judges have the authority to question whether the laws themselves are valid and just. Others argue that such fundamental probing overreaches judicial responsibility and extends judicial power into an area that should be the exclusive domain of the legislative branch of government.

Same-sex couples have taken their marriage cases to the courts in recent years in the hope that judges will find any exclusionary practice to be unjust discrimination. However, many who oppose gay marriage condemn recent judicial decisions that have given same-sex couples equal access to the rights and benefits of marriage. They argue that judges who change laws that are already in the books overstep the role of the judiciary. Among the critics is Senate majority leader Bill Frist (R-TN) who said, "Marriage should not be redefined by the courts. . . . We must protect, preserve and strengthen the institution of marriage against activist judges." By labeling some judges as "activists," opponents of gay marriage make it clear that, in their view, laws are only rightfully made by the citizens of the United States who voice their preferences by voting for legislators to represent them in Congress.

In contrast, gay marriage advocates compare judges' recent rulings in favor of gay marriage to the rulings judges made to rectify institutionalized racial discrimination during the civil rights struggles of earlier years. From their point of view, fighting for equality in the courts is a long-standing American tradition. Moreover, some advocates of gay marriage claim that judges are accused of being "activist" only when they support the rights of political or cultural minorities. Legal expert Steve Sanders writes:

> Many conservatives, full of phony populist indignation, tell a dishonest, oversimplified story [labeling judges as "activists"] to an ill-informed public. This provides cover for conservatives to appoint their own judges—many of whom are committed not to some tedious process of cranking the legal machinery, but rather to making law that reflects their policy preferences.

According to Sanders, some opponents of gay marriage only accuse judges of overstepping their role when judicial rulings do not meet with their approval. These smear campaigns, insists Sanders, cause "many Americans [to] confuse prejudice and sectarian dogma with legal reasoning."

State sovereignty versus national unity

Another key controversy in the gay marriage debate is the enduring issue of states' rights versus federal power. Since the founding of the republic, citizens have debated what balance of power should exist between individual states and the federal government. The movement to pass a federal amendment banning same-sex marriage has caused many Americans to question whether marriage issues should be resolved federally in the U.S. Constitution.

Objections to a federal amendment are not made exclusively by liberal Americans. Traditionally, conservative Americans tend to argue against sweeping federal directives that limit state self-government. Anti-federalists argue that each state should be able to determine its own policy on social issues such as marriage. To justify his support for a federal amendment as a Republican, President Bush explained that he believes the "voice of the people" is being compromised by the actions of a few judges in isolated cases. Such actions, he argues, potentially threaten every state in the union because of the "full faith and credit" clause in Article IV of the Constitution, which requires all states to honor the laws of every other state. "Those who want to change the meaning of marriage," said Bush, "will claim that this provision [the full faith and credit clause] requires all states and cities to recognize same-sex marriages performed anywhere in America."

Conservatives opposed to a federal resolution to the gay marriage issue cite a range of reasons. Some fear an amendment could divide the Republican Party and create deep resentment in those who think it is more important to focus on cutting taxes and reducing federal spending than battling over social issues such as marriage laws. Other Americans believe the Constitution should be amended only to address a great public policy need and always with the intent of strengthening and expanding rights and protections. They argue that an amendment that restricts marriage to heterosexuals limits rather than expands rights. Both conservative and liberal gay marriage advocates condemn the spirit of an amendment that they believe singles out one group of people for discrimination.

Separation of church and state

Perhaps the most contentious issue in the gay marriage debate is the meaning of the separation of church and state in the United States. Founding fathers Thomas Jefferson and James Madison fought vigorously to convince Constitutional Convention members in the 1780s that the government must be protected from any religious influences. Their efforts yielded Article VI, Section III in the Constitution ("No religious test shall ever be required as a qualification to any office or public trust under the United States") and the freedom-of-religion clause in the First Amendment of the Bill of Rights ("Congress shall make no law respecting an establishment of religion, or prohibiting the free exercise thereof").

As with the other key controversies about the role of government, the church/state issue is interpreted differently by opponents and advocates of gay marriage. Gay marriage foes such as the Catholic Congregation for the Doctrine of the Faith argue that state support of same-sex unions breaches freedom of religion and conscience. Their 2003 statement on gay marriage proclaims that "marriage is holy, while homosexual acts go against the natural moral law," and that no religious authority should be forced to conduct marriages that go against the organization's beliefs. According to the Catholic Congregation, legalizing gay marriage is the equivalent of religious persecution.

However, advocates of gay marriage point out that marriage is a civil institution as well as a religious one. Because the church and state are separate institutions, they argue, same-sex couples have a right to a marriage that is sanctioned by the government. Advocates emphasize that recent judicial decisions and legislation in support of gay marriage do not require religious organizations to conduct gay wedding ceremonies. Congressman Jesse L. Jackson Jr. criticizes those who want to make the gay marriage issue an exclusively moral or religious debate. He states, "All issues have a moral underpinning and a religious dimension to them, but in our secular society, religious institutions are under no moral, religious or legal obligation to perform or bless gay unions. Such institutions are free to either grant or withhold such celebrations and blessings." Like Jackson, political commentator Katha Pollitt believes that in a free republic like the United States, civil rights should be shared equally by all citizens regardless of their religious affiliation. She writes, "It's not about what God blesses, it's about what the government permits."

Advocates also challenge the notion that all religious groups oppose gay marriage and assert that those that do not should have the freedom to allow gay weddings complete with marriage licenses. The Universal Fellowship of Metropolitan Community Churches (UFMCC) has conducted gay and lesbian weddings since its inception in 1968. Similarly, the Unitarian Universalist Association passed a resolution in 1984 to affirm and conduct same-sex union ceremonies, and another in 1996 to support "legal recognition for marriage between members of the same sex." Many ministers, priests, rabbis, and other religious leaders have publicly conducted same-sex union ceremonies in recent years. Some have defied the official sanctions against gay unions in their own religious organizations and have spoken out for religious freedom in a diverse nation.

Clearly, the role of government in the gay marriage issue is a complex political and legal quagmire that raises fundamental questions about justice in the United States. Related questions about morality, family relationships, freedom of expression, and sexuality are also at stake in the gay marriage debate. *At Issue: Gay Marriage* includes a broad spectrum of views on the subject. The collection of voices in this volume reflects the debate over one of the most controversial issues facing Americans today.

1

A Legal History of Same-Sex Marriage Battles in the United States

NOLO Law for All

NOLO Law for All is a publisher of legal information to enable people to handle their own everyday legal matters. The company currently publishes A Legal Guide for Lesbian and Gay Couples.

Same-sex couples in the United States have been attempting to achieve legal recognition for their unions since the early 1970s. Gay and lesbian couples applied for marriage licenses, adoption privileges, and spousal immigration rights, but had little success in achieving legal recognition of their partnerships. By the mid-1980s homosexual couples began to focus on obtaining "domestic partnership" rights and benefits from employers and local governments. In the new millennium, marriage has resurfaced as a legal goal for same-sex couples. However, not all gays and lesbians support the drive to legalize same-sex marriage. In spite of the division, supporters of same-sex marriage have made some progress in their efforts to legalize it.

According to *Webster's New Collegiate Dictionary*, a family is "the basic unit in society having as its nucleus two or more adults living together and cooperating in the care and rearing of their own or adopted children." Despite this all-inclusive definition, a lesbian or gay couple—with or without children—is not the image conjured up when most people create a picture of a family.

Nevertheless, lesbian and gay couples (and their children) consider themselves families. And over the past several decades, same-sex couples have sought societal recognition of their families. It began in the early 1970s, when lesbian and gay couples applied for marriage licenses, asked courts to allow one partner to adopt the other, and took other steps to legally cement their relationships. Most of these efforts failed.

By the mid-1980s, the emphasis changed to seeking "domestic partnership" recognition for same-sex couples from both municipalities and private companies. This effort continued, with increasing strength, in the 1990s. And the desire to marry has again emerged. Some couples are applying to the state for marriage licenses and suing their states when their requests are denied. In Vermont, one such lawsuit resulted in the creation of a state law that permits same-sex couples to register their partnership as a "civil union," which entitles them to all the rights and benefits granted to married couples.

> **❝** *The lesbian and gay community is itself divided over the marriage issue.* **❞**

It's interesting to note that the lesbian and gay community is itself divided over the marriage issue. The community consists of an enormous number of people of every conceivable age, race, religion, lifestyle, income and opinion. It is, of course, impossible to convince such a large and diverse group of people to throw their political weight behind any one issue. For example, some argue that regardless of any individual's desire to get married, the community as a whole should support official recognition of their right to do so. On the other hand, there are those who decry marriage as a sexist and patriarchal institution that should be avoided at all costs. Still others are enjoying a higher level of economic prosperity than the average American and don't feel constrained in any way by a lack of marriage rights. Another group doesn't want to risk repercussions while perhaps another group just doesn't care one way or the other.

In 1978, the United States Supreme Court declared marriage

to be "of fundamental importance to all individuals" (*Zablocki v. Redhail*). The court described marriage as "one of the 'basic civil rights of man'" and "the most important relation in life." The court also noted that "the right to marry is part of the fundamental 'right to privacy'" in the U.S. Constitution.

Although marriage has been declared a fundamental right, no state yet recognizes same-sex marriages. Some states have passed laws specifically barring same-sex marriages, and the number of states with such laws is increasing. In recent years, the best news in the fight for recognition of same-sex unions came from Vermont, when the Vermont Supreme Court [in the 1999 *Baker v. State* case] ordered its state legislature to come up with a system providing same-sex couples with traditional marriage benefits and protections.

In response to the Supreme Court's mandate, the Vermont legislature passed the Vermont Civil Union law, which went into effect on July 1, 2000. While this law doesn't legalize same-sex marriages, it does provide gay and lesbian couples with many of the same advantages, including:

- use of family laws such as annulment, divorce, child custody, child support, alimony, domestic violence, adoption and property division
- the right to sue for wrongful death, loss of consortium and any other tort or law related to spousal relationships
- medical rights such as hospital visitation, notification and durable power of attorney
- family leave benefits
- joint state tax filing, and
- property inheritance without a will.

These rights apply only to couples residing in Vermont. And even for Vermont residents, this new civil union law does not provide same-sex couples with rights and benefits provided by federal law—for example, same-sex couples cannot take advantage of Social Security benefits, immigration privileges and the marriage exemption to federal estate tax.

It's too soon to tell what effect the Vermont Civil Union law will have on the nation. The law allows couples that aren't Vermont residents to register their civil unions in Vermont, but it is doubtful that other states will recognize their status. (However, two other states, California and Hawaii, have already passed comprehensive domestic partnership laws offering benefits similar to those available in Vermont.) Although the U.S. Constitution requires each state to give "full faith and credit" to the laws of other states—for example, by recognizing marriages and divorces made across state lines—the federal Defense of Marriage Act (DOMA), passed in 1996, expressly undercuts the full faith and credit requirement in the case of same-sex marriages. Because of the apparent conflict between the DOMA and the Constitution, equal rights advocates and their opponents would like to get a case before the U.S. Supreme Court to decide the issue of same-sex marriage once and for all. . . .

History of same-sex marriage attempts

Here's a chronological history of same-sex marriages cases decided prior to *Baker v. State.*

Baker v. Nelson (Minnesota, 1971). A gay male couple argued that the absence of sex-specific language in the Minnesota statute was evidence of the legislature's intent to authorize same-sex marriages. The couple also claimed that prohibiting them from marrying was a denial of their due process and equal protection rights under the Constitution. The court simply stated "we do not find support for [these arguments] in any decision of the United States Supreme Court."

Jones v. Hallahan (Kentucky, 1973). A lesbian couple argued that denying them a marriage license deprived them of three basic constitutional rights—the right to marry, the right to associate and the right to freely exercise their religion. The court refused to address the constitutional issues, holding that "the relationship proposed does not authorize the issuance of a marriage license because what they propose is not a marriage."

Singer v. Hara (Washington, 1974). A gay male couple argued that denying them the right to marry violated the state's Equal Rights Amendment (ERA). The court disagreed, holding that the purpose of the statute was to overcome discriminatory legal treatment as between men and women "on account of sex."

Adams v. Howerton (Colorado, 1975). The couple, a male American citizen and a male Australian citizen, challenged the Board of Immigration Appeals refusal to recognize their marriage for the purpose of the Australian obtaining U.S. residency as the spouse of an American. (The couple participated in a marriage ceremony with a Colorado minister and had been granted a marriage license by the Boulder, Colorado county clerk.)

First, the court ruled that the word "spouse" ordinarily means someone not of the same sex. Then the court looked at the 1965 amendments to the Immigration Act which expressly barred persons "afflicted with sexual deviations" (homosexuals) from entry into this country. The court concluded that it was unlikely that Congress intended to permit homosexual marriages for purposes of qualifying as a spouse of a citizen, when amendments to that section explicitly bar homosexuals from entering into the U.S.

> *Prohibiting them from marrying was a denial of their due process and equal protection rights under the Constitution.*

Thorton v. Timmers (Ohio, 1975). A lesbian couple sought a marriage license. In denying their request that the court order the clerk to issue them a license, the court concluded that "it is the express legislative intent that those persons who may be joined in marriage must be of different sexes."

De Santo v. Barnsley (Pennsylvania, 1984). When this couple split up, De Santo sued Barnsley for divorce, claiming that the couple had a common-law marriage. A common-law marriage is one where the partners live together, intend to be married and hold themselves out as married, without going through a formal marriage ceremony. Only a handful of states recognize common-law marriages—Pennsylvania is one of those states. The court threw the case out, stating that if the Pennsylvania common-law statute is to be expanded to include same-sex couples, the legislature will have to make that change.

Matter of Estate of Cooper (New York, 1990). Cooper died, leaving the bulk of his property to his ex-lover. His current lover sued to inherit as a "surviving spouse" under New York's inheritance laws. The court concluded that only a lawfully recognized husband or wife qualifies as a "surviving spouse" and that "persons of the same sex have no constitutional rights to enter into a marriage with each other."

Dean v. District of Columbia (Washington, DC, 1995). Two men sued the District of Columbia for the right to get married. They lost their case at the lower level and appealed. They lost again at the appellate level when the court decided, under current D.C. laws, that the district can refuse to grant marriage licenses to same-sex couples.

Baehr v. Miike (Hawaii, 1999). A nine-year battle over the issue of same-sex marriages ended just eleven days before the Vermont ruling in *Baker v. State*, discussed above. The plaintiff in the Baehr case argued that Hawaii's marriage license rules were discriminatory. The case set off a national debate over same-sex marriage rights and prompted an onslaught of state and federal legislation designed to preempt the possibility that other states would be forced to recognize same-sex marriages from Hawaii. The case was finally dismissed on the grounds that the legislature had passed a prohibition on same-sex marriages before the Hawaii Supreme Court could render a favorable opinion.

In general, recent years have been marked by a rapid succession of victories and disappointments for those seeking to legalize same-sex marriage. The best we can tell you now is, "Stay tuned."

2

Gay Marriage Should Be Legal

John Kusch

John Kusch is a writer and Internet developer who maintains a personal online log titled Letters from a Strip of Dirt *focusing on various cultural and political issues. He has written extensively about equality for gay and lesbian Americans.*

It is difficult to answer the question of who should define and enforce marriage. On the one hand, the government has the power to grant married people certain privileges and to demand that couples fulfill certain responsibilities such as fostering family stability. Various religions, on the other hand, define marriage as a sacrament in the context of spiritual life. Society also stakes a claim on the institution of marriage as a means to help families survive through tradition and social pressure. Because marriage is not a single institution with one definition, it is unfair to deny gay couples the right to marry. Instead, the state should legalize same-sex unions in order to honor existing social relationships that already function as marriages.

Today [August 21, 2003] you will likely be presented with an avalanche of figures and statistics on the topic of same-sex marriage, including polls demonstrating what percentage of the public is either in support or opposition, surveys estimating the number of same-sex households in the United States, studies claiming that the percentage of gay and lesbian Americans is ten percent or twenty percent or two percent, and speculative pieces on the potential effects of same-sex marriage on

John Kusch, testimony before the Wisconsin Joint Legislative Committee, August 21, 2003.

children, homes, religions and society as a whole.[1] As British politician George Canning once said, "I can prove anything by statistics—except the truth."

The truth, it seems to me, is that a matter like same-sex marriage, which involves civil rights, religious freedoms, and the sanctity of familial ties, should not be a matter of opinion polls. Instead of attempting to persuade this committee with facts and figures, I would rather inform the committee by telling the story of an unconventional marriage without which I would not be here today. Of course, I'm speaking of my parents.

Another story of the right to marry

In 1969, my mother was in the difficult position of being a Catholic divorcée with six children to fend for. Even today she would have struggled despite the governmental and community resources available to single mothers, but at the time her situation was truly desperate.

> *From the Catholic viewpoint at that time, my parents' union was not merely an objectionable marriage: it was a contradiction in terms.*

Luckily, my mother met a strong, loving, hardworking man, also a Catholic, who was willing to take her as his wife and take on her six children as his own. The man who would become my father, had an unshakeable belief in the importance of family loyalty that I still admire to this day. Such men were and are rare.

Yet despite their obvious love for one another and their willingness to accept both the joys and the responsibilities of family life, my parents were still Catholics, and the Church refused to annul my mother's previous marriage. [This despite the fact that her first husband physically abused her, engaged in flagrant adultery, and inadequately provided for her and her children.] According to Catholic teachings, they were forbid-

---

1. This was presented as testimony before the Wisconsin Joint Legislative Committee to express opposition to the Assembly Bill 475/Senate Bill 233 "Defense of Marriage Act."

den to marry, as their relationship violated the proscriptions against sex outside marriage. From the Catholic viewpoint at that time, my parents' union was not merely an objectionable marriage: it was a contradiction in terms. It was, simply, not a marriage. Through the lens of the Church, their relationship— their family—was reduced to a sex act.

The irony is not lost on me when today my relationship is compared by certain religious persons to various degrading sex acts.

Unable to marry in a Catholic ceremony, my parents were instead married before a judge, and the following year, I was born. Despite the Catholic position that my parents were not actually married and that I was an illegitimate child, I had two loving parents who cared and provided for me, along with my older brothers and sisters. We weren't a family, yet we were a family. As a child, I was understandably confused.

As an adult, I understand that the reason my parents were allowed to marry is that the government rightly understood that despite certain religious objections, my parents had voluntarily entered into a committed familial relationship, forming close bonds of kinship and interdependence, and that as a family it was in their best interest and thus in the interest of the greater community that their union have financial and legal stability that would allow them to support, protect and nurture one another and their children. Furthermore, the government understood that just as my parents were unable to force the Church to bless their union, no individual or group could prevent their union on purely religious grounds. In this way, the government respected the right of religion to define and enforce moral standards among its members while also respecting the right of individuals to adhere to moral standards of their own.

Without this compact of respect between government, religion, and the individual, a marriage like that of my parents—a marriage without which I might not have ended up here before you today—would never have been possible.

Does marriage belong to the government, religion, or the people?

It seems to me that the legislation currently under consideration by this committee raises a difficult question: Who owns marriage? In other words, who defines marriage, who allows marriage, and who enforces it? One possible answer is that the government owns it by virtue of its power to enact legislation that grants married persons certain privileges while charging them with certain responsibilities. Another answer is that religions own marriage, as each faith develops certain ceremonies and traditions that seek to define marriage in the context of spiritual life. Yet another answer is that society owns marriage, through its natural tendency to organize itself in ways that help families survive and to enforce those survival strategies through tradition and social pressure.

> *Government can fully represent a broad spectrum of citizens while at the same time respecting the sovereignty of religion and the needs of society.*

Yet any one of these answers seems to come up short in the face of such an old and weighty institution. Is marriage a sacrament, a contract, or a social condition? As someone who has had ample opportunity to ponder the meaning of marriage, I am led to believe that marriage not only falls under multiple ownership, but that marriage itself cannot be called a single institution.

Consider for example my parents who, having forgone a religious ceremony, still enjoyed the legal benefits of marriage and were considered a married couple by their peers. Consider also the couple who are joined in a religious ceremony and who function as a married couple in their community, but who for whatever reason do not register their union with the state. And in the case of same-sex marriage, consider the growing number of same-sex couples who consider themselves married, whose extended families and social peers consider them married, whose local governments consider them married, and whose employers consider them married—all despite the fact that according to the state and federal government (as well as several major religions), their marriage is a legal and spiritual impossibility.

Marriage has changed over time

These examples demonstrate that marriage already enjoys a wide range of definitions and applications, and that ownership of the marriage contract does not and cannot reside in any one governmental, religious, or social body. While it cannot be denied that the concept of same-sex marriage is a new (and for many people revolutionary) concept, proponents of same-sex marriage do not demand a change in the definition of marriage so much as an acknowledgement from the governing bodies that represent them that the definition of marriage has already changed.

It is perfectly understandable that certain groups and individuals, distressed at what they perceive as the erosion of a sacred religious vow, would seek to protect it by using the power of government to prevent further change. Yet to wield the power of government in order to enforce a singular and inflexible definition of marriage would satisfy some at the cost of disenfranchising a significant and growing segment of the population for whom marriage is a very different institution from what it was a decade or a century ago.

Those of us who strive for the legalization of same-sex marriage believe that government can fully represent a broad spectrum of citizens while at the same time respecting the sovereignty of religion and the needs of society. While we assert our right to participate in civic life and to form our own families and our own communities, we understand that our civil liberties do not entitle us to force our way through church doors or to demand societal approval or religious sanction. Those dialogues must be entered into on a local scale—church by church, community by community. . . .

At issue today is the foundation of what we call civil society. Is it possible for the government to respect my choice of mate—in my case, another man—despite the fact that parts of society might disagree with that choice? And if not, is it then appropriate that a distant cousin of mine could qualify as next of kin, whereas my partner of three years could not? My parents contradicted convention and religious teachings in order to give me a safe, stable home life. I am here today to ask each of you to consider that I might deserve a chance to try to be the husband my father was the day he married my mother.

3

Gay Marriage Should Not Be Legal

Congregation for the Doctrine of the Faith

The Congregation for the Doctrine of the Faith is the branch of the Vatican whose purpose is to promote doctrine that defends Christian traditions.

Granting legal recognition to gay unions would harm society on several levels. First, legal recognition of gay couples would legitimize immoral unions. Further, gay marriage would ultimately undermine marriage as the basis of a stable society. Since gay unions cannot produce children through natural and proper procreation, such unions do not contribute to the survival of the human race. Moreover, it is immoral to legitimize gay unions because it is not in the best interests of the children who might be adopted by gay couples. These children would be deprived of either the experience of motherhood or fatherhood. Because cohabiting homosexuals can make use of various legal provisions to protect their rights, there is no need to allow gay couples the legal status of marriage, especially since such a change would threaten the common good.

To understand why it is necessary to oppose legal recognition of homosexual unions, ethical considerations of different orders need to be taken into consideration.

From the order of right reason

The scope of the civil law is certainly more limited than that of the moral law, but civil law cannot contradict right reason with-

Congregation for the Doctrine of the Faith, "Considerations Regarding Proposals to Give Legal Recognition to Unions Between Homosexual Persons," www.vatican.va, July 31, 2003.

out losing its binding force on conscience. Every humanly-created law is legitimate insofar as it is consistent with the natural moral law, recognized by right reason, and insofar as it respects the inalienable rights of every person. Laws in favour of homosexual unions are contrary to right reason because they confer legal guarantees, analogous to those granted to marriage, to unions between persons of the same sex. Given the values at stake in this question, the State could not grant legal standing to such unions without failing in its duty to promote and defend marriage as an institution essential to the common good.

It might be asked how a law can be contrary to the common good if it does not impose any particular kind of behaviour, but simply gives legal recognition to a *de facto* reality which does not seem to cause injustice to anyone. In this area, one needs first to reflect on the difference between homosexual behaviour as a private phenomenon and the same behaviour as a relationship in society, foreseen and approved by the law, to the point where it becomes one of the institutions in the legal structure. This second phenomenon is not only more serious, but also assumes a more wide-reaching and profound influence, and would result in changes to the entire organization of society, contrary to the common good. Civil laws are structuring principles of man's life in society, for good or for ill. [As Pope John Paul II declared,] they "play a very important and sometimes decisive role in influencing patterns of thought and behaviour". Lifestyles and the underlying presuppositions these express not only externally shape the life of society, but also tend to modify the younger generation's perception and evaluation of forms of behaviour. Legal recognition of homosexual unions would obscure certain basic moral values and cause a devaluation of the institution of marriage.

From the biological and anthropological order

Homosexual unions are totally lacking in the biological and anthropological elements of marriage and family which would be the basis, on the level of reason, for granting them legal recognition. Such unions are not able to contribute in a proper way to the procreation and survival of the human race. The possibility of using recently discovered methods of artificial reproduction, beyond involving a grave lack of respect for human dignity, does nothing to alter this inadequacy.

Homosexual unions are also totally lacking in the conjugal

dimension, which represents the human and ordered form of sexuality. Sexual relations are human when and insofar as they express and promote the mutual assistance of the sexes in marriage and are open to the transmission of new life.

> *Allowing children to be adopted by persons living in such unions would actually mean doing violence to these children.*

As experience has shown, the absence of sexual complementarity in these unions creates obstacles in the normal development of children who would be placed in the care of such persons. They would be deprived of the experience of either fatherhood or motherhood. Allowing children to be adopted by persons living in such unions would actually mean doing violence to these children, in the sense that their condition of dependency would be used to place them in an environment that is not conducive to their full human development. This is gravely immoral and in open contradiction to the principle, recognized also in the United Nations Convention on the Rights of the Child, that the best interests of the child, as the weaker and more vulnerable party, are to be the paramount consideration in every case.

From the social order

Society owes its continued survival to the family, founded on marriage. The inevitable consequence of legal recognition of homosexual unions would be the redefinition of marriage, which would become, in its legal status, an institution devoid of essential reference to factors linked to heterosexuality; for example, procreation and raising children. If, from the legal standpoint, marriage between a man and a woman were to be considered just one possible form of marriage, the concept of marriage would undergo a radical transformation, with grave detriment to the common good. By putting homosexual unions on a legal plane analogous to that of marriage and the family, the State acts arbitrarily and in contradiction with its duties.

The principles of respect and non-discrimination cannot be invoked to support legal recognition of homosexual unions.

Differentiating between persons or refusing social recognition or benefits is unacceptable only when it is contrary to justice. The denial of the social and legal status of marriage to forms of cohabitation that are not and cannot be marital is not opposed to justice; on the contrary, justice requires it.

Nor can the principle of the proper autonomy of the individual be reasonably invoked. It is one thing to maintain that individual citizens may freely engage in those activities that interest them and that this falls within the common civil right to freedom; it is something quite different to hold that activities which do not represent a significant or positive contribution to the development of the human person in society can receive specific and categorical legal recognition by the State. Not even in a remote analogous sense do homosexual unions fulfil the purpose for which marriage and family deserve specific categorical recognition. On the contrary, there are good reasons for holding that such unions are harmful to the proper development of human society, especially if their impact on society were to increase.

From the legal order

Because married couples ensure the succession of generations and are therefore eminently within the public interest, civil law grants them institutional recognition. Homosexual unions, on the other hand, do not need specific attention from the legal standpoint since they do not exercise this function for the common good.

Nor is the argument valid according to which legal recognition of homosexual unions is necessary to avoid situations in which cohabiting homosexual persons, simply because they live together, might be deprived of real recognition of their rights as persons and citizens. In reality, they can always make use of the provisions of law—like all citizens from the standpoint of their private autonomy—to protect their rights in matters of common interest. It would be gravely unjust to sacrifice the common good and just laws on the family in order to protect personal goods that can and must be guaranteed in ways that do not harm the body of society.

4

Gay Marriage Would Promote Social Stability

Samuel G. Freedman

Samuel G. Freedman is a professor of journalism at Colum-bia University and is a regular contributor to USA Today, Rolling Stone, *and* Salon.com. *He has written several award-winning books, including* Jew vs. Jew: The Struggle for the Soul of American Jewry.

Although many conservatives argue otherwise, legalizing gay marriage would enhance the social stability of the United States. Marriage is an inherently conservative institution that requires a deeper commitment to civic and family responsibilities than unmarried couples undertake. It would only benefit the country to facilitate that level of commitment for more couples, including gay and lesbian couples. Accepting gay marriage as a civil right does not impinge on the rights of those who are morally or religiously opposed to it. Separation of church and state is a principle that allows Americans to support liberties and opportunities for all, even if they choose to live according to different values than those of their neighbors.

Seven summers ago, my wife and I took our children to the first wedding of their young lives. In a sun-dappled courtyard, before witnesses ranging from swaddled infants to a 93-year-old, my literary agent exchanged rings and vows with his gay lover, an author. Then I drank so much champagne my wife had to drive us home.

On that June afternoon in 1996, the ritual carried no legal weight, no assurance of inheritance or even spousal health coverage. Still, I had wanted my children to attend the ceremony, because it offered a vision of the tolerant future I hoped would be theirs.

Now, as the nation stands at the threshold of openly, seriously deciding whether to legalize gay marriage, that future is at hand.

The debate promises to be intense, protracted and ugly. At its end, the social stability of the country would be well-served by permitting gays and lesbians to join in formal domestic partnerships. Gay marriage, endorsed by the state, rewards a strain of social conservatism that benefits families, schools, workplaces and congregations.

A decade ago, we bungled a comparable opportunity. When the issue of gays in the military arose, the Clinton administration framed the policy known as "don't ask, don't tell." That supposed compromise in fact served to reinforce the closeting of homosexuals in the military. We should have built a monument to the gays and lesbians who had given their lives in the armed forces; we should have honored them for making the ultimate sacrifice of any citizen.

Similarly, if gays and lesbians want to make the public commitment to lifelong union, then that decision deserves the support of the law. As imperfectly as we practice it, marriage nonetheless connotes responsibilities and obligations beyond those of the unattached individual or of the couple, whether gay or straight, who simply live together.

A history of harmful discrimination

Centuries, literally millennia, of opposition to homosexuality have done nothing to extinguish it, because, whether as a matter of biology or psychology, it is plainly part of the human equation. What the slanders and excommunications and hate crimes have accomplished is to drive homosexuality underground, or into some vague limbo in which daily life is a stilted exercise in don't ask, don't tell.

Nearing 50, I am old enough to have seen the tormenting of "homos" in high school and the self-torture of gay teachers never free to acknowledge their sexuality. I remember the silence that descended over a group of my college friends one evening in the mid-1970s, when one mentioned he had a gay brother in San Francisco. In our respectful muteness, we reacted as if that brother had terminal cancer. Even when gays achieved cool in the '80s, they were exoticized, by others and by themselves.

The AIDS epidemic took hold and spread in America largely because gay male culture found its expression in the anonymous sex and multiple partners of the bathhouse scene. As if to compensate for straight society's refusal to allow them the prosaic forms of domesticity, many gay men disparaged monogamy itself as a boring heterosexual chore.

> **History tells us the years ahead will be bitter and difficult, but history also tells us progress will occur.**

It took some of the heroes of the AIDS crisis, such as author-activist Larry Kramer, to articulate a gay identity built around more than promiscuity. And it should come as no surprise that one of the most persuasive advocates for gay marriage is columnist Andrew Sullivan, a resolute Tory [conservative] on most political issues. A common thread of conservatism joins those positions.

But in the broader public debate now burgeoning, the conservative stance shapes up to be a definition of marriage that precludes homosexuals. Even after the adoption of anti-discrimination legislation protecting gays and lesbians in many states and cities, even after the extension of pension and health benefits by numerous public and private employers to homosexual couples, even after the emergence of gay TV stars and shows, the prospect of marriage stirs some ancient fears and hatreds.

Like the *Brown v. Board of Education* [ending racial segregation in public schools] decision nearly a half-century ago, the Supreme Court's recent ruling [on June 26, 2003, in *Lawrence v. Texas*] establishing a right to privacy for homosexuals has simultaneously pointed the way to equality and excited feverish opposition to it. History tells us the years ahead will be bitter and difficult, but history also tells us progress will occur.

Along with demagogues and bigots and opportunists, millions of men and women of principle and piety deplore the movement toward same-sex marriage. They must realize that their own moral opposition to it can coexist with federal or state statutes permitting it. The Catholic Church deems divorce a sin even as civil law allows it. Orthodox and Conservative Jewish rabbis will not perform interfaith wedding ceremonies even as half of American Jews marry gentiles.

Practicing a religion means joining a voluntary association and choosing to abide by its doctrines. Observers of America as far back as [French writer Alexis] de Toqueville have ascribed a good deal of our vigorous public life to the freedom of church and state from one another. Let it be so on the matter of gay marriage.

Personally, I can't help remembering that my agent and his partner had their commitment ceremony on the back steps of a church, an image of almost-ness. Seven years and two months later, they remain together, a middle-aged married couple in the eyes of their friends and colleagues, but still not their country.

5

Gay Marriage Would Harm Society

Sam Schulman

Sam Schulman is a New York writer whose work appears in Commentary *magazine, the* New York Press, *and the* Jewish World Review, *among other magazines.*

In recent years opponents of gay marriage have lost influence because their arguments fall short of the mark. Ultimately, the reason to protect traditional heterosexual marriage is to prevent the alteration of fundamental unwritten laws that organize human society. The essence of marriage is not love, fidelity, financial security, or any of the other characteristics often associated with marriage. Marriage venerates and guides the joining of men and women—a joining that is the only connection capable of creating life. Without marriage, society would resort to a social order based on polygamy.

The feeling seems to be growing that gay marriage is inevitably coming our way in the U.S., perhaps through a combination of judicial fiat and legislation in individual states. Growing, too, is the sense of a shift in the climate of opinion. The American public seems to be in the process of changing its mind not actually in favor of gay marriage, but toward a position of slightly revolted tolerance for the idea. Survey results suggest that people have forgotten why they were so opposed to the notion even as recently as a few years ago.

It is curious that this has happened so quickly. With honorable exceptions, most of those who are passionately on the side of the traditional understanding of marriage appear to be at a loss for words to justify their passion; as for the rest, many seem to wish gay marriage had never been proposed in the first place, but also to have resigned themselves to whatever happens. In this respect, the gay-marriage debate is very different from the abortion debate, in which few with an opinion on either side have been so disengaged.

I think I understand why this is the case: as someone passionately and instinctively opposed to the idea of homosexual marriage, I have found myself disappointed by the arguments I have seen advanced against it. The strongest of these arguments predict measurable harm to the family and to our arrangements for the upbringing and well-being of children. I do not doubt the accuracy of those arguments. But they do not seem to get at the heart of the matter.

Gay marriage will topple the foundation of society

To me, what is at stake in this debate is not only the potential unhappiness of children, grave as that is; it is our ability to maintain the most basic components of our humanity. I believe, in fact, that we are at an "Antigone[1] moment." Some of our fellow citizens wish to impose a radically new understanding upon laws and institutions that are both very old and fundamental to our organization as individuals and as a society. As Antigone said to Creon, we are being asked to tamper with "unwritten and unfailing laws, not of now, nor of yesterday; they always live, and no one knows their origin in time." I suspect, moreover, that everyone knows this is the case, and that, paradoxically, this very awareness of just how much is at stake is what may have induced, in defenders of those same "unwritten and unfailing laws" a kind of paralysis.

Admittedly, it is very difficult to defend that which is both ancient and "unwritten"; the arguments do not resolve themselves into a neat parade of documentary evidence, research results, or citations from the legal literature. Admittedly, too, proponents of this radical new understanding have been uncommonly effective in presenting their program as something that is not radical at all but as requiring merely a slight and painless adjustment in our customary arrangements. Finally,

---

1. Antigone is a character in the Greek play *Antigone* by Sophocles. In the play, she defies King Creon's orders that ignored ancient traditions.

we have all learned to practice a certain deference to the pleas of minorities with a grievance, and in recent years no group has benefited more from this society-wide dispensation than homosexuals. Nevertheless, in the somewhat fragmentary notes that follow, I hope to re-articulate what I am persuaded everyone knows to be the case about marriage, and perhaps thereby encourage others with stronger arguments than mine to help break the general paralysis.

Examining arguments in favor of gay marriage

Let us begin by admiring the case *for* gay marriage. Unlike the case for completely unrestricted abortion, which has come to be something of an embarrassment even to those who advance it, the case for gay marriage enjoys the decided advantage of appealing to our better moral natures as well as to our reason. It deploys two arguments. The first centers on principles of justice and fairness and may be thought of as the civil-rights argument. The second is at once more personal and more utilitarian, emphasizing the degradation and unhappiness attendant upon the denial of gay marriage and, conversely, the human and social happiness that will flow from its legal establishment.

> *Advocates of gay marriage need no longer call upon the law to light (or force) the way; they need only ask it to ratify a trend.*

Both arguments have been set forth most persuasively by two gifted writers, Bruce Bawer and Andrew Sullivan, each of whom describes himself as a social conservative. In their separate ways, they have been campaigning for gay marriage for over a decade. Bawer's take on the subject is succinctly summarized in his 1993 book, *A Place at the Table;* Sullivan has held forth on the desirability of legalizing gay marriage in numerous articles, on his website (andrewsullivan.com), and in an influential book, *Virtually Normal* (1995).

The civil-rights argument goes like this. Marriage is a legal state conferring real, tangible benefits on those who participate in it: specifically, tax breaks as well as other advantages when it comes to inheritance, property ownership, and employment benefits. But family law, since it limits marriage to heterosexual couples over the age of consent, clearly discriminates against a segment of the population. It is thus a matter of simple justice that, in Sullivan's words, "all public (as opposed to private) discrimination against homosexuals be ended and that every right and responsibility that heterosexuals enjoy as public citizens be extended to those who grow up and find themselves emotionally different." Not to grant such rights, Sullivan maintains, is to impose on homosexuals a civil deprivation akin to that suffered by black Americans under Jim Crow.

> *▟▟ The modest request of gay-marriage advocates for 'a place at the table' is thus profoundly selfish. ▟▟*

The utilitarian argument is more subtle; just as the rights argument seems aimed mainly at liberals, this one seems mostly to have in mind the concerns of conservatives. In light of the disruptive, anarchic, violence-prone behavior of many homosexuals (the argument runs), why should we not encourage the formation of stable, long-term, monogamous relationships that will redound to the health of society as a whole? In the apt words of a letter-writer in *Commentary* [magazine] in 1996:

> Homosexual marriage . . . preserves and promotes a set of moral values that are essential to civilized society. Like heterosexual marriage, it sanctions loyalty, unselfishness, and sexual fidelity; it rejects the promiscuous, the self-serving, the transitory relationship. Given the choice between building family units and preventing them, any conservative should favor the former.

Bawer, for his part, has come close to saying that the inability of many male homosexuals to remain faithful in long-term relationships is a consequence of the lack of marriage rights—a burning sign of the more general stigma under which gays labor in our society and which can be redressed by changes in law. As it happens, though, this particular line of argument is already somewhat out of date and is gradually being phased out of the discussion. The toleration of gay styles of life has come about on its own in American society, without the help of legal sanctions, and protecting gay couples from the contempt of bigots is not the emergency Bawer has depicted. Quite the contrary: with increasing numbers of gay partners committing themselves to each other for life, in full and approving view of their families and friends, advocates of gay marriage need no longer call upon the law to light (or force) the way; they need only ask it to ratify a trend.

In brief, legalizing gay marriage would, in Andrew Sullivan's summary formulation, offer homosexuals the same deal society now offers heterosexuals: general social approval and specific legal advantages in exchange for a deeper and harder-to-extract-yourself-from commitment to another human being. Like straight marriage, it would foster social cohesion, emotional security, and economic prudence.

The case is elegant, and it is compelling. But it is not unanswerable. And answers have indeed been forthcoming, even if, as I indicated at the outset, many of them have tended to be couched somewhat defensively. Thus, rather than repudiating the very idea of an abstract "right" to marry, many upholders of the traditional definition of marriage tacitly concede such a right, only going on to suggest that denying it to a minority amounts to a lesser hurt than conferring it would impose on the majority, and especially on children, the weakest members of our society.

Homosexuality is incompatible with marriage

Others, to be sure, have attacked the Bawer/Sullivan line more forthrightly. In a September 2000 article in *Commentary*, "What Is Wrong with Gay Marriage," Stanley Kurtz challenged the central contention that marriage would do for gay men what it does for straights; i.e., "domesticate" their natural male impulse to promiscuity. Citing a number of academic "queer theorists" and radical gays, Kurtz wrote:

> In contrast to moderates and "conservatives" like Andrew Sullivan, who consistently play down [the] difference [between gays and straights] in order to promote their vision of gays as monogamists-in-the-making, radical gays have argued "more knowledgeably, more powerfully, and more vocally than any opponent of same-sex marriage would dare to do" that homosexuality, and particularly male ho-

mosexuality, is by its very nature incompatible with
the norms of traditional monogamous marriage.

True, Kurtz went on, such radical gays nevertheless support
same-sex marriage. But what motivates them is the hope of
"eventually undoing the institution [of marriage] altogether,"
by delegitimizing age-old understandings of the family and
thus (in the words of one such radical) "striking at the heart of
the organization of Western culture and societies."

> *The essence of marriage is to sanction and solemnize that connection of opposites which alone creates new life.*

Nor are radical gays the only ones to entertain such destructive ambitions. Queuing up behind them, Kurtz warned,
are the proponents of polygamy, polyandry, and polyamorism,
all ready to argue that their threesomes, foursomes, and other
"nontraditional" arrangements are entitled to the same rights
as everyone else's. In a recent piece in the *Weekly Standard*,
Kurtz has written that the "bottom" of this particular slippery
slope is "visible from where we stand":

> Advocacy of legalized polygamy is growing. A net-
> work of grass-roots organizations seeking legal
> recognition for group marriage already exists. The
> cause of legalized group marriage is championed
> by a powerful faction of family-law specialists. In-
> fluential legal bodies in both the United States and
> Canada have presented radical programs of mari-
> tal reform, . . . [even] the abolition of marriage.
> The ideas behind this movement have already
> achieved surprising influence with a prominent
> American politician [Al Gore].

Like other critics of same-sex marriage, Kurtz has himself
been vigorously criticized, especially by Sullivan. But he is almost certainly correct as to political and legal realities. If we
grant rights to one group because they have demanded "which
is, practically, how legalized gay marriage will come to pass" we
will find it exceedingly awkward to deny similar rights to oth-

ers ready with their own dossiers of "victimization." In time, restricting marriage rights to couples, whether straight or gay, can be made to seem no less arbitrary than the practice of restricting marriage rights to one man and one woman. Ultimately, the same must go for incestuous relationships between consenting adults; a theme to which I will return.

Traditional heterosexual marriage preserves the family

A different defense of heterosexual marriage has proceeded by circling the wagons around the institution itself. According to this school of thought, ably represented by the columnist Maggie Gallagher, the essential purpose of that institution is to create stable families:

> Most men and women are powerfully drawn to perform a sexual act that can and does generate life. Marriage is our attempt to reconcile and harmonize the erotic, social, sexual, and financial needs of men and women with the needs of their partner and their children.

Even childless marriages protect this purpose, writes Gallagher, by ensuring that, as long as the marriage exists, neither the childless husband nor the childless wife is likely to father or mother children outside of wedlock.

Gallagher is especially strong on the larger, social meaning of heterosexual marriage, which she calls "inherently normative":

> The laws of marriage do not create marriage, but in societies ruled by law they help trace the boundaries and sustain the public meanings of marriage. . . . Without this shared, public aspect, perpetuated generation after generation, marriage becomes what its critics say it is: a mere contract, a vessel with no particular content, one of a menu of sexual lifestyles, of no fundamental importance to anyone outside a given relationship.

Human relationships are by nature difficult enough, Gallagher reminds us, which is why communities must do all they can to strengthen and not to weaken those institutions that keep us up to a mark we may not be able to achieve through our own efforts. The consequences of not doing so will be an intensification of all the other woes of which we have so far had only a taste in our society and which are reflected in the galloping statistics of illegitimacy, cohabitation, divorce, and fatherlessness. For Gallagher, the modest request of gay-marriage advocates for "a place at the table" is thus profoundly selfish as well as utterly destructive, for gay marriage would require society at large to gut marriage of its central presumptions about family in order to accommodate a few adults' "desires."

James Q. Wilson, Maggie Gallagher, Stanley Kurtz, and others, including William J. Bennett in *The Broken Hearth* (2001) are right to point to the deleterious private and public consequences of instituting gay marriage. Why, then, do their arguments fail to satisfy completely? Partly, no doubt, it is because the damage they describe is largely prospective and to that degree hypothetical; partly, as I remarked early on, the defensive tone that invariably enters into these polemics may rob them of the force they would otherwise have. I hardly mean to deprecate that tone: anyone with homosexual friends or relatives, especially those participating in longstanding romantic relationships, must feel abashed to find himself saying, in effect, "You gentlemen, you ladies, are at one and the same time a fine example of fidelity and mutual attachment" and the thin edge of the wedge; Nevertheless, in demanding the right to marry, that is exactly what they are.

The true nature of marriage

To grasp what is at the other edge of that wedge—that is, what stands to be undone by gay marriage—we have to distinguish marriage itself from a variety of other goods and values with which it is regularly associated by its defenders and its aspirants alike. Those values—love and monogamous sex and establishing a home, fidelity, childbearing and childrearing, stability, inheritance, tax breaks, and all the rest—are not the same as marriage. True, a good marriage generally contains them, a bad marriage is generally deficient in them, and in law, religion, and custom, even under the strictest of moral regimes, their absence can be grounds for ending the union. But the essence of marriage resides elsewhere, and those who seek to arrange a kind of marriage for the inherently unmarriageable are looking for those things in the wrong place.

The largest fallacy of all arises from the emphasis on romantic love. In a book published last year [2002], Tipper and [former vice president] Al Gore defined a family as those who are "joined at the heart"—"getting beyond words, legal formalities, and even blood ties." The distinction the Gores draw in this sentimental and offhand way is crucial, but they utterly misconstrue it. Hearts can indeed love, and stop loving. But what exactly does this have to do with marriage, which can follow, precede, or remain wholly independent of that condition?

It is a truism that many married people feel little sexual or romantic attraction to each other—perhaps because they have been married too long, or perhaps, as some men have always claimed, because the death of sexual desire is coincident with the wedding ceremony. ("All comedies are ended by a marriage," [the poet] Byron wittily and sadly remarked.) Many people in ages past, certainly most people have married for reasons other than sexual or romantic attraction. So what? I could marry a woman I did not love, a woman I did not feel sexually attracted to or want to sleep with, and our marriage would still be a marriage, not just legally but in its essence.

The truth is banal, circular, but finally unavoidable: by definition, the essence of marriage is to sanction and solemnize that connection of opposites which alone creates new life. (Whether or not a given married couple does in fact create new life is immaterial.) Men and women *can* marry only because they belong to different, opposite, sexes. In marriage, they surrender those separate and different sexual allegiances, coming together to form a new entity. Their union is not a formalizing of romantic love but represents a certain idea—a construction, an abstract thought—about how best to formalize the human condition. This thought, embodied in a promise or a contract, is what holds marriage together, and the creation of this idea of marriage marks a key moment in the history of human development, a triumph over the alternative idea, which is concubinage.

6

Same-Sex Marriage Would Benefit Children

Anne Pollock

Anne Pollock is a graduate student in history and social studies of science and technology at the Massachusetts Institute of Technology (MIT). She writes for the Thistle, *a progressive student newspaper at MIT.*

Antigay activists claim that they are fighting to protect children whenever they propose legislation against gay marriage. However, it is children who are hurt by "defense of marriage" amendments that exclusively limit marriage to heterosexual couples. Gay and lesbian families include children of all ages who are forced to live without the legal rights and benefits of other children with married parents. The first priority of civil marriage should be to provide a secure environment for *all* children. The religious right's claim that children benefit from their assaults against gay families is nothing less than hypocritical.

It's called a "Super-DOMA." If you haven't been following anti-gay politics, the name might not ring a bell. Super-DOMA sounds like it could be a comic book hero—or a comic book villain. It's actually an anti-gay constitutional amendment afoot here in Massachusetts, working its way through the state legislature. It is called Super-DOMA because it is more extreme than the federal Defense of Marriage Act (DOMA) that [President Bill] Clinton signed into law in 1996. By putting anti-same-sex-marriage wording right into the state constitution, the proponents of the amendment hope to prevent any legal recognition of same-sex relationships in Massachusetts forever. Besides the mean-spiritedness of denying us rights we don't even have, this amendment could be mobilized to undercut the gains we have already made and be a serious roadblock on our path toward full human rights.

Here is the text of the proposed amendment:

> It being the public policy of this Commonwealth to protect the unique relationship of marriage in order to promote among other goals, the stability and welfare of society and the best interests of children, only the union of one man and one woman shall be valid or recognized as a marriage in Massachusetts. Any other relationship shall not be recognized as a marriage or its legal equivalent. (Text of proposed Amendment H 3190)

Massachusetts is not the first state to have a "Defense of Marriage" amendment before the legislature, and it won't be the last. One of the tricky things about the "Defense of Marriage" approach is the way that it uses positive language, making the amendment seem like a positive move rather than an exclusionary one. The amendment doesn't name names, so how do we know who its target is? Easy: [lesbian, bisexual, gay, and transgendered (LBGT)] families are the ones seeking legal recognition. There is not a social movement in Massachusetts for legalized polygamy, and the specification of "legal equivalent" is a clear move against civil unions of the kind available to same-sex couples in Vermont.

Children deserve to have their families recognized

Same-sex marriage used to strike me as a rather conservative, assimilationist thing to demand. I used to think, hey, leave the state-sanctioned domesticity to the straight people, no skin off my nose. But now I see the need for lesbians, gays, and bisexuals to have that choice. Not only do I think it's okay if marriage makes people feel happy and accepted, but LBGT families deserve access to the wide range of legal protections marriage can offer—from greater access to health insurance to property sharing to inheritance to hospital visitation. Moreover, all these rights and responsibilities become even more important when we have kids.

The Super-DOMA makes it sound like LBGTs don't have children. I suppose the fantasy is that refusing to recognize the relationships within which we have children will somehow prevent us from having them. But queer families exist. Like it or not, we are having children in all kinds of ways. Those children are harmed if their families aren't legally recognized. Second-parent adoption, and health-care proxy forms, and wills, and legal contracts are possible in Massachusetts. But not only do they not quite accomplish as much as marriage does, they are very cumbersome and expensive, and this amendment might even serve as grounds to challenge them. Allowing civil marriage wouldn't make queer families perfectly stable—obviously it doesn't do that for the heterosexuals—but it would help those who chose to do so to formalize our relationships with each other and our children so that through thick and thin we know where we stand and what our rights and responsibilities are.

The Super-DOMA being proposed for Massachusetts doesn't say anything about religion. Indeed, civil marriage is not and should not be about religion. It should have something to do with what is best for children and society. Talk with children of gays, lesbians, and bisexuals and you'll find that, as far as they're concerned, denying their families' legal recognition just doesn't make sense. It is important that we not let the religious right claim that they are speaking on behalf of the children, since they ignore the kids directly affected by anti-gay legislation.

So what to do in the face of Super-DOMA? The first thing to do, after being aware of it, is to stand against it at every level. That means contacting state legislators now, hoping to prevent its passage there. If it passes the legislature, it will appear before Massachusetts voters. Part of the importance of public awareness about it now is to be ready if it does appear on the ballot: people need to know that it is not about protecting straight families, but about attacking LBGT ones. They need to know that voting "no" is voting "yes" to openness in Massachusetts. Fight the Super-DOMA, spread the love.[1]

---

1. The proposed Massachusetts constitutional amendment known as "Super-DOMA" was rejected at the Massachusetts Constitutional Convention on July 17, 2003.

7

Same-Sex Marriage Would Harm Children

Maggie Gallagher

Maggie Gallagher is a nationally syndicated columnist and a leading voice in the new marriage movement. She is the author of several books on marriage, including The Case for Marriage: Why Married People Are Happier, Healthier, and Better-Off Financially.

Marriage is much more than simply publicly celebrating private relationships of love. The essence of marriage is to preserve a traditional family structure to guide the one relationship that can produce children— the sexual relationship between a woman and a man. First and foremost, children need stable families to become the kind of adults who will in turn provide stable families for their future children. Civilized society quickly deteriorates without this continuation of responsible family organization. Legalizing same-sex marriage would sanction families that would deprive children of the experience of either motherhood or fatherhood.

G ay marriage is no longer a theoretical issue. Canada has it. Massachusetts is expected to get it any day.[1] The Goodridge decision there could set off a legal, political, and cultural battle in the courts of 50 states and in the U.S. Congress. Every politician, every judge, every citizen has to decide: Does same-

1. On November 18, 2003, three months after this article was published, the Massachusetts Supreme Court ruled that same-sex couples are legally entitled to marry under the state constitution.

sex marriage matter? If so, how and why?

The timing could not be worse. Marriage is in crisis, as everyone knows: High rates of divorce and illegitimacy have eroded marriage norms and created millions of fatherless children, whole neighborhoods where lifelong marriage is no longer customary, driving up poverty, crime, teen pregnancy, welfare dependency, drug abuse, and mental and physical health problems. And yet, amid the broader negative trends, recent signs point to a modest but significant recovery.

The good news about marriage

Divorce rates appear to have declined a little from historic highs; illegitimacy rates, after doubling every decade from 1960 to 1990, appear to have leveled off, albeit at a high level (33 percent of American births are to unmarried women); teen pregnancy and sexual activity are down; the proportion of home-making mothers is up; marital fertility appears to be on the rise. Research suggests that married adults are more committed to marital permanence than they were twenty years ago. A new generation of children of divorce appears on the brink of making a commitment to lifelong marriage. In 1977, 55 percent of American teenagers thought a divorce should be harder to get; in 2001, 75 percent did.

> *Now the time has come to decide: Will unisex marriage help or hurt marriage as a social institution?*

A new marriage movement—a distinctively American phenomenon—has been born. The scholarly consensus on the importance of marriage has broadened and deepened; it is now the conventional wisdom among child welfare organizations. As a Child Trends research brief summed up: "Research clearly demonstrates that family structure matters for children, and the family structure that helps children the most is a family headed by two biological parents in a low-conflict marriage. Children in single-parent families, children born to unmarried mothers, and children in stepfamilies or cohabiting relationships face higher risks of poor outcomes. . . . There is thus value for children in promoting strong, stable marriages between biological parents."

What will court-imposed gay marriage do to this incipient recovery of marriage? For, even as support for marriage in general has been rising, the gay marriage debate has proceeded on a separate track. Now the time has come to decide: Will unisex marriage help or hurt marriage as a social institution?

> **What has happened is not a flowering of libertarian freedom, but a breakdown of social and civic order that can reach frightening proportions.**

Why should it do either, some may ask? How can Bill and Bob's marriage hurt Mary and Joe? In an exchange with me in the just-released book "Marriage and Same Sex Unions: A Debate," Evan Wolfson, chief legal strategist for same-sex marriage in the Hawaii case, Baer v. Lewin, argues there is "enough marriage to share." What counts, he says, "is not family structure, but the quality of dedication, commitment, self-sacrifice, and love in the household."

Family structure does not count. Then what is marriage for? Why have laws about it? Why care whether people get married or stay married? Do children need mothers and fathers, or will any sort of family do? When the sexual desires of adults clash with the interests of children, which carries more weight, socially and legally?

These are the questions that same-sex marriage raises. Our answers will affect not only gay and lesbian families, but marriage as a whole.

In ordering gay marriage on June 10, 2003, the highest court in Ontario, Canada, explicitly endorsed a brand new vision of marriage along the lines Wolfson suggests: "Marriage is, without dispute, one of the most significant forms of personal relationships. . . . Through the institution of marriage, individuals can publicly express their love and commitment to each other. Through this institution, society publicly recognizes expressions of love and commitment between individuals, granting them respect and legitimacy as a couple."

The Ontario court views marriage as a kind of Good Housekeeping Seal of Approval that government stamps on certain registered intimacies because, well, for no particular reason the court can articulate except that society likes to recognize expressions of love and commitment. In this view, endorsement of gay marriage is a no-brainer, for nothing really important rides on whether anyone gets married or stays married. Marriage is merely individual expressive conduct, and there is no obvious reason why some individuals' expression of gay love should hurt other individuals' expressions of non-gay love.

Marriage is a foundation of society

There is, however, a different view—indeed, a view that is radically opposed to this: Marriage is the fundamental, cross-cultural institution for bridging the male-female divide so that children have loving, committed mothers and fathers. Marriage is inherently normative: It is about holding out a certain kind of relationship as a social ideal, especially when there are children involved. Marriage is not simply an artifact of law; neither is it a mere delivery mechanism for a set of legal benefits that might as well be shared more broadly. The laws of marriage do not create marriage, but in societies ruled by law they help trace the boundaries and sustain the public meanings of marriage.

In other words, while individuals freely choose to enter marriage, society upholds the marriage option, formalizes its definition, and surrounds it with norms and reinforcements, so we can raise boys and girls who aspire to become the kind of men and women who can make successful marriages. Without this shared, public aspect, perpetuated generation after generation, marriage becomes what its critics say it is: a mere contract, a vessel with no particular content, one of a menu of sexual lifestyles, of no fundamental importance to anyone outside a given relationship.

The marriage idea is that children need mothers and fathers, that societies need babies, and that adults have an obligation to shape their sexual behavior so as to give their children stable families in which to grow up.

Which view of marriage is true? We have seen what has happened in our communities where marriage norms have failed. What has happened is not a flowering of libertarian freedom, but a breakdown of social and civic order that can reach frightening proportions. When law and culture retreat from sustaining the marriage idea, individuals cannot create marriage on their own.

In a complex society governed by positive law, social institutions require both social and legal support. To use an analogy, the government does not create private property. But to make a market system a reality requires the assistance of law as well as culture. People have to be raised to respect the property of others, and to value the trait of entrepreneurship, and to be law-abiding generally. The law cannot allow individuals to define for themselves what private property (or law-abiding conduct) means. The boundaries of certain institutions (such as the corporation) also need to be defined legally, and the definitions become socially shared knowledge. We need a shared system of meaning, publicly enforced, if market-based economies are to do their magic and individuals are to maximize their opportunities.

Successful social institutions generally function without people's having to think very much about how they work. But when a social institution is contested—as marriage is today—it becomes critically important to think and speak clearly about its public meanings.

Again, what is marriage for? Marriage is a virtually universal human institution. In all the wildly rich and various cultures flung throughout the ecosphere, in society after society, whether tribal or complex, and however bizarre, human beings have created systems of publicly approved sexual union between men and women that entail well-defined responsibilities of mothers and fathers. Not all these marriage systems look like our own, which is rooted in a fusion of Greek, Roman, Jewish, and Christian culture. Yet everywhere, in isolated mountain valleys, parched deserts, jungle thickets, and broad plains, people have come up with some version of this thing called marriage. Why?

It all comes down to kids

Because sex between men and women makes babies, that's why. Even today, in our technologically advanced contraceptive culture, half of all pregnancies are unintended: Sex between men and women *still* makes babies. Most men and women are powerfully drawn to perform a sexual act that can and does generate life. Marriage is our attempt to reconcile and harmonize the erotic, social, sexual, and financial needs of men and women with the need of their partner and their children.

How to reconcile the needs of children with the sexual desires of adults? Every society has to face that question, and some resolve it in ways that inflict horrendous cruelty on children born outside marriage. Some cultures decide these children don't matter: Men can have all the sex they want, and any children they create outside of marriage will be throwaway kids; marriage is for citizens—slaves and peasants need not apply. You can see a version of this elitist vision of marriage emerging in America under cover of acceptance of family diversity. Marriage will continue to exist as the social advantage of elite communities. The poor and the working class? Who cares whether their kids have dads? We can always import people from abroad to fill our need for disciplined, educated workers.

Our better tradition, and the only one consistent with democratic principles, is to hold up a single ideal for all parents, which is ultimately based on our deep cultural commitment to the equal dignity and social worth of all children. All kids need and deserve a married mom and dad. All parents are supposed to at least try to behave in ways that will give their own children this important protection. Privately, religiously, emotionally, individually, marriage may have many meanings. But this is the core of its public, shared meaning: Marriage is the place where having children is not only tolerated but welcomed and encouraged, because it gives children mothers and fathers.

The value of successful marriage

Of course, many couples fail to live up to this ideal. Many of the things men and women have to do to sustain their own marriages, and a culture of marriage, are *hard*. Few people will do them consistently if the larger culture does not affirm the critical importance of marriage as a social institution. Why stick out a frustrating relationship, turn down a tempting new love, abstain from sex outside marriage, or even take pains not to conceive children out of wedlock if family structure does not matter? If marriage is not a shared norm, and if successful marriage is not socially valued, do not expect it to survive as the generally accepted context for raising children. If marriage is just a way of publicly celebrating private love, then there is no need to encourage couples to stick it out for the sake of the children. If family structure does not matter, why have marriage laws at all? Do adults, or do they not, have a basic obligation to control their desires so that children can have mothers and fathers?

The problem with endorsing gay marriage is not that it would allow a handful of people to choose alternative family forms, but that it would require society at large to gut marriage of its central presumptions about family in order to accommodate a few adults' desires.

The debate over same-sex marriage, then, is not some sideline discussion. It *is* the marriage debate. Either we win—or we lose the central meaning of marriage. The great threat unisex marriage poses to marriage as a social institution is not some distant or nearby slippery slope, it is an abyss at our feet. If we cannot explain why unisex marriage is, in itself, a disaster, we have already lost the marriage ideal.

> *If marriage is just a way of publicly celebrating private love, then there is no need to encourage couples to stick it out for the sake of the children.*

Same-sex marriage would enshrine in law a public judgment that the desire of adults for families of choice outweighs the need of children for mothers and fathers. It would give sanction and approval to the creation of a motherless or fatherless family as a deliberately chosen "good." It would mean the law was neutral as to whether children had mothers and fathers. Motherless and fatherless families would be deemed just fine.

Same-sex marriage advocates are startlingly clear on this point. Marriage law, they repeatedly claim, has nothing to do with babies or procreation or getting mothers and fathers for children. In forcing the state legislature to create civil unions for gay couples, the high court of Vermont explicitly ruled that marriage in the state of Vermont has nothing to do with procreation. Evan Wolfson made the same point in "Marriage and Same Sex Unions": "Isn't having the law pretend that there is only one family model that works (let alone exists) a lie?" He goes on to say that in law, "marriage is not just about procreation—indeed is not necessarily about procreation at all."

Wolfson is right that in the course of the sexual revolution the Supreme Court struck down many legal features designed to reinforce the connection of marriage to babies. The animus of elites (including legal elites) against the marriage idea is not brand new. It stretches back at least thirty years. That is part of the problem we face, part of the reason 40 percent of our children are growing up without their fathers.

Keeping it in the family

It is also true, as gay-marriage advocates note, that we impose no fertility tests for marriage: Infertile and older couples marry, and not every fertile couple chooses procreation. But every marriage between a man and a woman is capable of giving any child they create or adopt a mother and a father. Every marriage between a man and a woman discourages either from creating fatherless children outside the marriage vow. In this sense, neither older married couples nor childless husbands and wives publicly challenge or dilute the core meaning of marriage. Even when a man marries an older woman and they do not adopt, his marriage helps protect children. How? His marriage means if he keeps his vows, that he will not produce out-of-wedlock children.

Does marriage discriminate against gays and lesbians? Formally speaking, no. There are no sexual-orientation tests for marriage; many gays and lesbians do choose to marry members of the opposite sex, and some of these unions succeed. Our laws do not require a person to marry the individual to whom he or she is most erotically attracted, so long as he or she is willing to promise sexual fidelity, mutual caretaking, and shared parenting of any children of the marriage.

But marriage is unsuited to the wants and desires of many gays and lesbians, precisely because it is designed to bridge the male-female divide and sustain the idea that children need mothers and fathers. To make a marriage, what you need is a husband and a wife. Redefining marriage so that it suits gays and lesbians would require fundamentally changing our legal, public, and social conception of what marriage is in ways that threaten its core public purposes.

Some who criticize the refusal to embrace gay marriage liken it to the outlawing of interracial marriage, but the analogy is woefully false. The Supreme Court overturned anti-miscegenation laws because they frustrated the core purpose of marriage in order to sustain a racist legal order. Marriage laws, by contrast, were not invented to express animus toward homosexuals or anyone else. Their purpose is not negative, but positive: They uphold an institution that developed, over thousands of years, in thousands of cultures, to help direct the erotic desires of men and women into a relatively narrow but indispensably fruitful channel. We need men and women to marry and make babies for our society to survive. We have no similar public stake in any other family form—in the union of same-sex couples or the singleness of single moms.

Meanwhile, *cui bono*? To meet the desires of whom would we put our most basic social institution at risk? No good research on the marriage intentions of homosexual people exists. For what it's worth, the Census Bureau reports that 0.5 percent of households now consist of same-sex partners. To get a proxy for how many gay couples would avail themselves of the health insurance benefits marriage can provide, I asked the top 10 companies listed on the Human Rights Campaign's website as providing same-sex insurance benefits how many of their employees use this option. Only one company, General Motors, released its data. Out of 1.3 million employees, 166 claimed benefits for a same-sex partner, *one one-hundredth of one percent.*

People who argue for creating gay marriage do so in the name of high ideals: justice, compassion, fairness. Their sincerity is not in question. Nevertheless, to take the already troubled institution most responsible for the protection of children and throw out its most basic presumption in order to further adult interests in sexual freedom would not be high-minded. It would be morally callous and socially irresponsible.

If we cannot stand and defend this ground, then face it: The marriage debate is over. . . . We lost.

8

A Constitutional Amendment Against Gay Marriage Is Wrong

Dale Carpenter

Dale Carpenter is a professor at the University of Minnesota Law School and writes the column "Outright" for several gay publications, including the Texas Triangle, OutSmart, *and* PlanetOut.

There are four convincing reasons to oppose a constitutional amendment defining marriage as exclusively heterosexual. In the first place, a federal amendment is unnecessary because it is unlikely that the Supreme Court would declare same-sex marriage a constitutional right. Next, a constitutional amendment would undermine federalism since family law has always been the province of the states. Moreover, such an amendment would be undemocratic because it would limit state powers to affirm individual rights. Finally, imposing a federal amendment is an overreaction to the unlikely event of court-imposed gay marriage.

It's time to start marshaling our arguments against the Federal Marriage Amendment (FMA). The FMA, which has now [in 2003] been introduced in the House of Representatives, would define marriage in the United States as the union of one man and one woman. It would henceforth ban gay marriages (and other forms of legal recognition of gay couples) throughout the country—at least until the amendment could be repealed,

Dale Carpenter, "Four Reasons to Oppose the Federal Marriage Amendment," www.TxTriangle.com, October 24–30, 2003. Copyright © 2003 by The Texas Triangle Online. Reproduced by permission of the author.

something that has happened only once in more than two centuries of constitutional history. Passage of the FMA would set back the cause of gay marriage for perhaps 25–50 years, possibly for the lifetime of most people reading this column.

The theory of the FMA seems to be that the states must be saved from themselves, from their own legislatures, from their own courts, and from their own people, lest they formally recognize gay relationships. Whatever one thinks of same-sex marriage as a matter of policy, no person who cares about our Constitution should support this amendment. It is unnecessary, contrary to the structure of our federal system, anti-democratic in a peculiar way, and a form of overkill.

The central argument against the FMA is that allowing gay marriage would be a good thing, for gays and society. But here are four arguments against the FMA that even an opponent of gay marriage should be able to accept:

First, a constitutional amendment is unnecessary. It is a solution in search of a problem. No state in the union has yet recognized same-sex marriages. Even if and when a state court approved same-sex marriage in its own jurisdiction, that can and should be a matter for a state to resolve internally, through its own governmental processes, as in fact the states have been doing.

> *The FMA is constitutional overkill. It is like hauling out a sledgehammer to kill a gnat.*

Supporters of the FMA argue that the Constitution's Full Faith and Credit Clause might be used to impose gay marriage on the country. That clause requires each state to give "full faith and credit" to the "public acts, records and judicial proceedings" of other states. But this clause has never been interpreted to mean that every state must recognize every marriage performed in every other state. Each state may refuse to recognize a marriage performed in another state if that marriage would violate the state's public policy. Thirty-seven states have already declared it is their public policy not to recognize same-sex marriages.

It is also unlikely the Supreme Court or the federal appellate courts, for the foreseeable future, would declare a constitutional right to same-sex marriage. *Lawrence v. Texas*, the recent [2003] sodomy decision, does not change this. Lawrence involved the most private of acts (sexual conduct) in the most private of places (the home); by contrast, marriage is a public institution freighted with public meaning and significance. If I gave my first year constitutional law students an exam question asking them to distinguish Lawrence from a decision favoring same-sex marriage, I am very confident they could do so.

Moreover, if the Court were suddenly to order nationwide same-sex marriage it would be taking on the entire country, something it almost never does. We should not tamper with the Constitution to deal with hypothetical questions as if it were part of some national law school classroom.

States should control family law

Second, a constitutional amendment would be a radical intrusion on federalism. States have traditionally controlled their own family law. The nation's commitment to this federalism is enshrined in our Constitution's very structure.

But federalism is not valuable simply as a tradition. It has a practical benefit. It allows the states to experiment with public policies, to determine whether they work. That is happening right now. States are trying a variety of approaches to test whether encouraging stable same-sex unions is, on balance, a good or bad thing.

Repudiating our history, the FMA would prohibit state courts or even state legislatures from authorizing same-sex marriages. It might even prevent state courts from enforcing domestic partnership or civil union laws.

An amendment would interfere with the democratic process

Third, the FMA would be peculiarly anti-democratic. Simple majority rule is the strong presumption of democracies. But, as conservative legal scholar Bruce Fein recently wrote, "that presumption and its purposes would be defeated by the constitutional rigidity and finality of a no-same-sex-marriage amendment."

While all constitutional amendments constrain democratic politics, the FMA would mark the first time in the nation's history the Constitution was amended to limit democratic decisions designed to make the states more inclusive and more affirming of individual rights. The FMA reflects a deeply anti-democratic impulse, a fundamental distrust of normal political processes.

Fourth, the FMA is constitutional overkill. It is like hauling out a sledgehammer to kill a gnat. Even if I have been wrong about the imminent likelihood of a court-imposed gay marriage revolution, the FMA is not a carefully tailored response to that problem. A much narrower amendment, dealing only with preserving state's control on the issue, could be proposed. Even such a narrower amendment, however, would be unnecessary.

In sum, the FMA is not a response to any problem we currently have. Never before in the history of the country have we amended the Constitution in response to a threatened or actual state court decision. Never before have we adopted a constitutional amendment to limit the states' ability to control their own family law. Never before have we amended the Constitution to restrict the ability of the democratic process to expand individual rights. This is no time to start.

9

A Constitutional Amendment Against Gay Marriage Is Necessary

First Things

First Things *is published by the Institute on Religion and Public Life, a research and education institute focusing on religious perspectives of public issues.*

Gay marriage activists are gaining ground by forcing the issue into state courts and legislatures and by pressuring the Supreme Court to rule in favor of gay marriage for the entire nation. A federal marriage amendment to the U.S. Constitution that defines marriage exclusively as a heterosexual union is necessary to prevent this national legalization of gay marriage. Allowing same-sex marriage will hurt children, who need the guidance and influence of both mothers and fathers. A federal amendment that protects traditional marriage is the only way to prevent the courts from taking democratic power from the American people who oppose gay marriage.

> Marriage in the United States shall consist only of the union of a man and a woman. Neither this Constitution or the constitution of any state, nor state or federal law, shall be construed to require that marital status or the legal incidents thereof be conferred on unmarried couples or groups.

That is the proposed amendment to the Constitution that is now gathering powerful support in the Congress and in several states. Prudent citizens are reluctant to amend the Constitution unless persuaded that it is necessary. What would become the twenty-eighth amendment is necessary because the courts are moving toward a de facto amendment of the Constitution that mandates the radical redefinition of marriage and family. The question before us is how the Constitution will be amended: by judicial fiat or by "We the People of the United States" employing the means established by the Constitution. Entailed in that question is whether change will serve to advance a social revolution unsought and unwanted by the American people or will serve to secure an institution essential to the well-being of our society. The Constitution will be amended, either by constitutional means or by activist judges [who advocate their causes on the bench] practicing what is aptly described as the judicial usurpation of politics.

The need for a federal marriage amendment

The proposed marriage amendment has been carefully crafted by leading constitutional scholars. The first sentence means that no legislature or court may confer the name of marriage on same-sex unions or recognize a same-sex marriage contracted in another country, such as Canada or the Netherlands. The second sentence is aimed more specifically at activist courts, both state and federal, preventing them from imposing same-sex marriage or its equivalent. The question of adopting arrangements other than marriage, such as civil unions, is left to the determination of the people through the democratic process in the several states. Where the people have had the opportunity to decide the question of same-sex marriage—in Hawaii and Alaska, for instance—they have decided against it, and have done so decisively.

A proper devotion to the principles of federalism has led some to question the amendment because, they say, it would "nationalize" marriage law. The nationalizing of marriage law, however, is precisely what the activists pressing for same-sex unions are on the edge of achieving. They hope that in the next few years same-sex marriage will be decreed by the Supreme Court. In addition, same-sex couples will travel to any state that allows them to marry or enter civil unions, and will then demand that their home states give "full faith and credit" to the judgment that recognizes their status. The great majority of same-sex couples contracting civil unions in Vermont, for instance, do not live in Vermont. They will be suing for recognition of their status in the courts of their home states. An additional and declared strategy is to attack the constitutionality of the Federal Defense of Marriage Act, overwhelmingly adopted by Congress in 1996. One way or another, federalism is compromised. The marriage amendment will establish a general rule against same-sex marriage while leaving the matter of contractual unions and other nonmarital arrangements to the states.

We have been brought to the present circumstance by the astonishing success of the homosexual movement over the past three decades. Traditionally, sodomy was viewed as an act, and was condemned as unnatural and deviant. A hundred years ago, homosexuality was viewed as a condition afflicting people who are prone to engaging in such unnatural and deviant acts. Today "gay" signifies not so much an act or condition as the identity of people who say that they most essentially are what they do and want to do sexually. The rhetorical and conceptual movement has been from act to condition to identity, bringing us to the demand for same-sex marriage. About two percent of the combined teenage and adult male population, and considerably less of the female, are said to be a minority deprived of their rights. In particular, they claim to be discriminated against in that they are "excluded" from the institution of marriage. They are not asking for tolerance of their private sexual practices and of the gay subculture constituted by such practices. They are demanding, rather, public acceptance and approval. That is the whole point of focusing on the status of marriage, which is a quintessentially public institution.

Do most gays want marriage?

It is by no means evident that most, or even many, gays are interested in entering into a legally recognized union. Until recently, more radical activists and proponents of "queer theory" vigorously opposed the movement for same-sex unions, arguing that gays should not surrender their erotic freedom to the constraints associated with the "bourgeois" institution of marriage. More recently, the radicals have lined up in support of same-sex marriage, joining the proponents of polygamy and "polyamory" who are now so influential, if not dominant, in the academic field of marriage and family law. We do not have to speculate about their aims. They have by now produced a large literature in support of what they themselves describe as a social revolution that would replace traditional marriage and family with a wide array of "family" arrangements constructed on the basis of expressive individualism and the maximizing of erotic options. A quarter century ago [1979], President Jimmy Carter convened the White House Conference on the Family, Under pressure from such radical ideologues, the name was changed to the White House Conference on Families, in the plural. The hour of the ideologues has now arrived, and they have rallied to the battle for same-sex marriage.

There are a few gays who express admiration for traditional marriage and say they simply want to be included in its benefits. They claim they are now excluded. And they are right. They are not excluded by others; they are excluded by their identity as gays. To be homosexual is a condition; to be gay is a decision. Some say no other decision is available to them, but that is not true. Sexual temptations, like other temptations, can be resisted. In many cases, sexual orientation can be changed. Human frailties notwithstanding, chastity is a possibility for all. Yet we are faced with a not-insignificant number of people who say that gay is who they are, whether by choice or by fate, and that they are unfairly excluded from the companionship, stability, and other goods of marriage. Were the Supreme Court to do their bidding tomorrow, however, they would still be excluded from marriage.

> *Sexual temptations, like other temptations, can be resisted. In many cases, sexual orientation can be changed.*

Throughout history and in all major cultures, marriage is a union between a man and a woman. That is what marriage is. A man and a man or a woman and a woman may have an intense but chaste friendship, including shared living arrangements. It is not the business of the state to certify or regulate friendships. As for those who choose a sexual relationship, we may well understand their yearning for public approval of their choice. But same-sex marriage is not marriage. It is at most a simulacrum of marriage, a poignant attempt to create a semblance of some features of marriage, a pretending to be something like the relationship between husband and wife that is marriage. The reality is not changed if the state collaborates in the pretense and calls it marriage.

To which some respond that it is a harmless pretense. If a very small minority so desperately want to be legally designated as married, even though everybody knows that their relationship is not really a marriage, why not let them? It seems the generous thing to do. It is further argued that such state-sanctioned unions would reduce the typically wild promiscuity that is characteristic of the gay lifestyle. Nobody can know whether same-sex marriage would, in fact, help domesticate the gay subculture. We do know, however, that it would radically change the customs, laws, and moral expectations embedded in millennia of human experience. Marriage and family law reflects the historically cumulative complexities of necessarily public concerns about property, inheritance, legal liability, and the legitimacy of children—the latter entailing a host of responsibilities for which parents, and especially men, can be held accountable. One of the most fundamental prerequisites of social order, it has been almost universally recognized, is the containment of the otherwise unbridled sexual activity of the human male, and marriage is—among the many other things that marriage is—the primary instrument of that necessary discipline.

Children come first

Marriage and family law is, above all, about children. Same-sex couples cannot from their sexual acts procreate children. Gay activists contend that that only makes their circumstance identical with that of a marriage in which the woman is beyond the child-bearing years. But that, too, is not true. A marriage between an older man and woman does not contradict the definition of marriage as a union between a man and a woman. In addition, such a marriage aims at preventing the man from having children by other women, which is, obviously, not a consideration in same-sex relations. The activists respond that gays can adopt children, which is legal in some jurisdictions. Here again the concern for children becomes paramount. After decades of experiments with single-parent families, "open marriages," and easy divorce, the evidence is in and there is today near-unanimous agreement on what should always have been obvious: judged by every index of well-being, there is no more important factor in the lives of children than having a mother and father in the home. Lesbians and gays in same-sex unions cannot be mothers and fathers, except in the poignant simulacrum of pretended sex roles. Given the ambiguities, uncertainties, and curiosities of children in coming to understand their sexuality, the Vatican's Congregation for the Doctrine of the Faith is surely right when it says in its recent statement that denying the child the experience of having a mother and father is a cruel deprivation.

> *// What is called homophobia is more accurately understood as a positive judgment regarding the common good. //*

Many oppose same-sex unions and the consequent revolution in marriage and family law because they believe homosexuality is a disorder and homosexual acts are morally wrong. That is not a private prejudice. It is not, as the Supreme Court has claimed, an "irrational animus." It is a considered and very public moral judgment grounded in clear reason and historical experience, and supported by the authority of the biblical tradition. Nobody should apologize for publicly advocating a position informed by the foundational moral truths of Western Civilization. Of course, those who do so will be accused of "homophobia." Homophobia is a term of recent coinage intended to serve as a conversation stopper. Its power to intimidate is rapidly diminishing. Support for the civilizational tradition in this regard is not a phobia; it is not an irrational fear. Concern about the legal establishment and normalization of sexual deviance is fully warranted. What is called homophobia is more accurately understood as a positive judgment regarding the common good and, most particularly, the well-being of children. It should not be, but it still is, necessary to add that hatred of gays or denial of their human or civil rights is evil and must be unequivocally condemned. Moreover, it must be candidly acknowledged that gay demands and agitations today are not unrelated to patterns of sexual hedonism in the general culture.

The faulty civil rights argument

The debate is now underway as to whether civil rights include the right of gays to have their relationships legally designated as marriage. There are many factors in the debate not addressed here. It is claimed, for instance, that a gay right to marriage is on a moral and legal continuum with extending rights to blacks and women. That convenient but simplistic comparison does not bear close examination. Discrimination against blacks and women was recognized, albeit too slowly, as contradicting the foundational values and institutions of our society. Those values were vindicated and those institutions strengthened by including people who had been unjustly excluded. The just demand of blacks and women was for full participation in the opportunities and responsibilities of the social order. The demand for gay marriage, by way of sharpest contrast, is premised upon the recognition that gays cannot participate in that order's most basic institution, and it is therefore aimed not at their inclusion but at the institution's deconstruction by redefinition. The humpty-dumpty logic is that, if you cannot do something you want to do, you redefine that something, turning it into something you can do. When such word games are translated into law, the public meaning of the something that most people can and want to do is radically changed. The public meaning of marriage and family—in law, and more gradually, in social customs and expectations—is changed for everybody. Gay activists can try but we do not think they will succeed in persuading most Americans that their marriages and families are the same thing that gays can and want to do.

> *It appears that the Supreme Court has quite forgotten the purpose and source of authority set forth by the Constitution.*

One factor that has been neglected to date is that, according to the reasoning of the recent Lawrence decision of the Supreme Court,[1] homosexuality will be viewed as a suspect category that, as in the case of race, will trigger a vast array of laws and regulations associated with the antidiscrimination regime. With respect to affirmative action, quota systems, rules about "hate

1. On June 26, 2003, the U.S. Supreme Court struck down Texas's "Homosexual Conduct" law in the *Lawrence and Garner v. Texas* decision. The "Homosexual Conduct" law had formerly criminalized oral and anal sex by consenting gay couples.

speech," and much else, attitudes and actions relating to gays will be subject to, in the language of the courts, "strict scrutiny." Minimally, this will mean that homosexuality and heterosexuality, marriage and the gay semblance of marriage, will in the public schools be presented on the basis of scrupulous equality. Since almost no parents want their children to be homosexual or gay, this prospect is likely to generate powerful resistance.

The courts vs. the people

Without the marriage amendment, the debate that is now underway may well be short-circuited by the courts. One way or another, the Constitution will be amended. If it is amended by the judiciary, as the Supreme Court did in its 1973 invention of an unlimited abortion license,[2] we will almost certainly enter upon a severe intensification of what is rightfully called the culture war. Lincoln forcefully stated in his first inaugural address that the American people are not prepared to surrender their right to self-government to even the most eminent tribunal. Whether that is still true of the American people is once again being put to the test.

Just government is derived from the consent of the governed, says the Declaration of Independence. In this democracy, consent means popular deliberation, debate, and decision through the representative polity established by the Constitution. In the Lawrence decision, Justice Anthony Kennedy, writing for the majority, invoked what Justice Antonin Scalia calls the "sweet mystery of life" passage from the 1992 Casey decision that affirmed the infamous Roe ruling on abortion: "At the heart of liberty is the right to define one's own concept of meaning, of the universe, and of the mystery of human life." In that way of thinking, the dominant, if not exclusive, purpose of the Constitution in dealing with rights is to serve the autonomous self as construed by the foundationless philosophy of expressive individualism. The moral, social, political, and legal order must bend to the individual definition of truth, no matter how willful or arbitrary. In support of that logic, the Lawrence opinion cites the authority of the above-mentioned ideologues and even of like-minded jurists in the European Union.

It appears that the Supreme Court has quite forgotten the

---

2. The *Roe v. Wade* decision established a woman's constitutional right to an abortion.

purpose and source of authority set forth by the Constitution. That purpose and source of authority is clearly stated in the Preamble: "We the people of the United States, in order to form a more perfect union, establish justice, insure domestic tranquility, provide for the common defense, promote the general welfare, and secure the blessings of liberty to ourselves and our posterity, do ordain and establish this Constitution for the United States of America."

We are now engaged in a great debate about whether same-sex marriage and the criminalizing of opposition to homosexuality and the gay agenda will serve to establish justice, ensure domestic tranquility, and promote the general welfare. (Provision for the common defense is, of course, relevant to the inclusion of gays in the military, which the logic of Lawrence would make mandatory.) Of crucial importance is the securing of liberty understood as what the Founders called the "ordered liberty" of a blessing bestowed, as distinct from the unbridled license of expressive individualism and the quest for the satisfaction of insatiable desire.

The marriage amendment might finally fail, but its passage by Congress and submission to the states for ratification can ensure that "We the People" will not be excluded from the deliberation and decisions that will determine the future of marriage and family, the most necessary of institutions in the right ordering of this or any society.

10

Canada's Same-Sex Marriage Law Should Not Be Opposed in the Name of Religion

Tarek Fatah and Nargis Tapal

Tarek Fatah is the host of the weekly TV show The Muslim Chronicle *in Toronto, Canada, and is a founding member of the Muslim Canadian Congress. Nargis Tapal writes short stories and poetry.*

The Canadian government submitted draft legislation to its supreme court in July 2003 that would include same-sex couples in the legal definition of civil marriage. However, the proposed law explicitly protects the right of religious organizations to refuse to perform same-sex marriages. Therefore, religious leaders have no reason to oppose the law. Civil laws are separated from religious practices specifically to ensure that all Canadians share the same civil rights in spite of differences in opinion or belief. Gay and lesbian couples deserve the same civil rights and benefits of marriage that heterosexual couples enjoy.

L ast month [August 2003], we attended a number of weddings in Toronto. Each had its own flavour, from Pakistani to Palestinian, from elaborate Orthodox church ceremonies to modest mosque rituals. Though the rites differed, the grooms and brides were all beaming with joy.

As these couples embraced their future together, we couldn't help but feel sad for Canada's gay and lesbian couples being pilloried for seeking the same happiness. We were also taken back to a humid August evening in Karachi in 1974 when we were permitted to marry.

Gays and lesbians wishing to marry face a gantlet of opposition and we, as a heterosexual Muslim couple, can empathize with their pain. To become husband and wife, we, too, had to confront deep-seated prejudices. Culture, religion, and family would not permit the daughter of a Shia Muslim of Gujarati ethnicity to marry the son of a Sunni Muslim of Punjabi ancestry.

Four years earlier, our paths had crossed at a noisy demonstration at the University of Karachi. Two 20-year-olds pursuing graduate studies in English literature; one, an orator with two stints as a political prisoner; the other, a Beatles fan with a Ringo Starr mop of hair, who had never been to a protest rally in her life. They fell in love. In true Islamic tradition, she proposed, he accepted.

However, it was not to be that easy. This was traditional Pakistan where nothing happened without parental assent. When news got out that Nargis Tapal and Tarek Fatah wanted to wed, all hell broke loose. Both families vetoed the match. Devastated, we contemplated eloping, and were accepted at Oklahoma State University, but just to get there would cost a fortune, and we were penniless.

With nowhere to run, we persevered and several years later, both sets of parents buckled and gave their consent. To this day, we still cannot understand why it was so difficult to achieve such simple joy. After 29 years as husband and wife, we want no one denied the happiness we enjoy.

Sadly, the gatekeepers of bliss and the purveyors of grief are still alive and well. From prelates and imams to rabbis and pundits, the forces of religion are arrayed against the gay and lesbian community. Once again, we are witnessing an attack on joy and happiness in the name of religion and tradition.

Religion vs. bigotry

As practising Muslims, we acknowledge that no faith, particularly Islam in its traditional interpretation, permits same-sex marriage or condones homosexuality. However, neither does faith allow hate and bigotry to be camouflaged as a quest for religious purity.

Most Canadian Muslims reject the notion of same-sex marriages and they are perfectly entitled to their beliefs, if, indeed, the issue is one of belief. But we think the position taken by religious leaders attacks the basic humanity of gays and lesbians. Dehumanizing "the other" is the first step to setting them as targets of bigotry and hate. Invoking religion to accomplish this task is shameful.

A Muslim monthly magazine asked its readers in an editorial, "Would you rather have church or state in your bedroom?"

> *If you believe your religion doesn't permit gay marriage, then simply don't marry a person of your own sex. End of story.*

Without answering the question, and oblivious to the implications of inviting church, mosque or state into our bedrooms, the writer goes on to predict moral disaster.

Accepting homosexual relationships as "marriage" will be the last nail in the coffin of human morality, according to the editorial. We Muslims allowed and promoted the delinquency in our daily life and kept quiet; we tolerated the illegitimate relationships of consenting adults outside marriage; we turned a blind eye to the "coming out of the closet" and hid behind the curtain of "hate the sin, but love the sinner.". . . Even if we are looked upon in the West as "fundamentalists" or "homophobes," it is an obligation for all Muslims to do our part just as the Catholics are doing.

Last nail in the coffin of human morality? Not the Holocaust, not the genocide in Rwanda, not the massacres in Bosnia? Just same-sex marriage? Not murder, not hunger, not rape, not war, not honour killing, not illiteracy, not sexual assault by clergy, not its cover-up? To the editorial writer, nothing seems to be as vile as homosexuality.

Tolerance should come first

Muslims should know better than to fall into this trap. They have been at the receiving end of slander and hate and it has taken collective action of some courageous people to defend the human rights and humanity of Muslims as equal citizens in our society. Even though an overwhelming majority of Canadians does not believe in the Qur'an as a word of God and Prophet Muhammad, may peace be upon him, as a Messenger of God, we Muslims have been given a status, at least in the law, as equal citizens, no matter how offensive others may find our religion.

The same holds true for the other side. After all, Muslims do not believe that Jesus was a Son of God; or that God should be worshipped in physical depictions such as statues; or that God does not exist at all, as atheists say. However, not only have we learned to accept Canadians with whom we have profound differences of religious belief, we have developed a society in which these differences are no hindrance to our relationship with each other.

It has been the intrinsically tolerant nature of Canadian society that has defined the rights of Muslims as equal citizens, despite our minority status. How can we then campaign against the very values that accord us the dignity we deserve?

If you believe your religion doesn't permit gay marriage, then simply don't marry a person of your own sex. End of story. Why would you wish to impose this standard on people who believe that religion, in their interpretation, does not exclude same-sex marriages?

The same religious groups that today say their only objection to the proposed law[1] is the word "marriage," were at the forefront of challenging Bob Rae's Bill 167 in 1994; a proposed law that did not mention same-sex marriage and spoke only of same-sex rights.

The law drafted by the federal government as presented to the Supreme Court makes an explicit declaration protecting the right of any church, mosque, synagogue, and temple to refuse to perform same-sex marriages.

So why the fuss over gay marriage? Could it be the same forces of religion, tradition, culture, and hate that opposed our heterosexual marriage 30 years ago are still making their presence felt? Is it joy that they fear? Happiness, it seems, is an affront; they simply cannot fathom the idea of two people wishing to live together as a family, and to be accepted the way the Almighty created them.

As a happily married Muslim couple who almost weren't,

---

1. On June 10, 2003, before this article was published, the Ontario Court of Appeals made same-sex marriage legal in Ontario. The proposed law referred to here is the drafted legislation to align same-sex marriage rights with the Canadian Charter of Rights and Freedoms. As part of the Ontario decision, the federal government was given until July 12, 2004, to amend the charter.

we need to speak on their behalf, even though Islam does not permit same-sex marriages. If gays and lesbians wish to pursue their own path in life, who are we to place obstacles in their way? If their choices are contrary to that of the Divine, only the Divine can be certain. Let us find God in our kindness and compassion instead of hate and self-righteousness. For isn't God the most merciful and the most compassionate?

Only God knows whether we are right in standing up for our gay friends, but we do so in all sincerity and with the hope that no one should shower grief over the happiness sought by another human being. Let us learn to live and let live.

11

Religion Will Be Undermined by the Massachusetts Same-Sex Marriage Law

David Limbaugh

David Limbaugh, brother of radio talk-show host Rush Limbaugh, is an attorney, politician, and writer. He is a regular contributor to WorldNetDaily.com and the Washington Times, *and he recently published the book* Persecution: How Liberals Are Waging Political War Against Christians.

Most of the recent legal decisions in favor of homosexual rights have claimed that it is wrong to "legislate morality." In actuality, the U.S. courts and federal government historically have based decisions on a moral code—specifically on a tradition of biblical moral beliefs. That long-standing convention has been undermined by decisions such as the Massachusetts Supreme Court ruling in favor of gay marriage, which puts the rights of individuals above the interest of the majority or the moral stability of society. By demolishing traditional marriage, extreme secularists are destroying the Judeo-Christian foundation of American culture.

Given the public outcry about the federal court's order for the removal of Judge Roy Moore's Ten Commandments display [from the Alabama state judicial building in 2002], I'm surprised there isn't as much alarm about the Massachusetts Supreme Court decision to sanctify gay marriage.

David Limbaugh, "Uprooting Our Biblical Foundation," www.townhall.com, November 21, 2003. Copyright © 2003 by David Limbaugh. Reproduced by permission.

In the Moore case you have a federal court telling a state court that it can't symbolically recognize the God of the Bible as the source of our laws (or otherwise). In the Massachusetts case you have a state court ruling that the Bible *can't be* the source of our laws. I think the latter has even graver implications.

Follow me on this. There is little question that the institution of marriage between a man and woman was ordained by the Bible.

> *Not only are our statutory and common law rooted in biblical morality; at a more fundamental level, so is our constitution.*

Genesis 2:24 says, "Therefore shall a man leave his father and his mother, and shall cleave unto his wife: and they shall be one flesh." That is a prescription for man and woman to be joined, not man and man or woman and woman.

The Massachusetts Court ruled that because the Massachusetts Constitution "affirms the dignity and equality of all individuals" and "forbids the creation of second-class citizens," homosexuals have a right to marry.

The individual vs. society

This should be no surprise, as it is a result of a logical progression in our jurisprudence toward radical individualism—the rights of the individual trump everything else—including the interest of the majority in establishing a moral and stable society.

Since the United States Supreme Court in its recent [2003] sodomy case (*Lawrence vs. Texas*[1]) reaffirmed the Court's earlier pronouncement that "Our obligation is to define the liberty of all, not to mandate our own moral code," it's hardly a surprise that a state court is following suit. The Massachusetts court is doing precisely that: forbidding the state legislature from mandating a moral code—at least one with Biblical roots.

The oft-repeated lie that "we can't legislate morality" has finally born its poisonous fruit. Of course we can legislate moral-

1. The *Lawrence and Garner v. Texas* decision ruled 6-3 that sodomy laws are unconstitutional.

ity. We always have. We must. Try looking at the criminal code of any state or the federal system and tell me it isn't based on morality. Look further into our civil law and try to deny that much, if not most, of tort law [dealing with civil wrongs resulting in injury or harm] and contract law, not to mention property law, are rooted in our traditional (Biblical) moral beliefs.

It is not just for mercantile reasons that men are prohibited from breaching contracts. And punitive damages in tort law are awarded not to compensate the victim, but to punish the tortfeasor [perpetrator]. Punishment—that's a moral concept.

The danger to religious liberty

Not only are our statutory and common law rooted in biblical morality; at a more fundamental level, so is our constitution. If we remove that foundation, the fabric of our society will unravel, and we'll eventually lose our liberties—ironically, at the hands of those claiming to champion freedom. And, by the way, the Massachusetts Supreme Court, in demolishing traditional marriage, is itself legislating—that's right, I said "legislating," not "adjudicating," morality.

Secularists in our culture and on our courts are not just turning the First Amendment Establishment Clause[2] on its head and using it as a weapon to smother religious liberty for Christians. They are further attacking our Judeo-Christian foundation by promoting individualism to the extreme—to the exclusion of Biblical truths.

In the abortion cases, the mother's personal convenience taken to an obscene extreme trumps the very right to life of the baby made in God's image. In the Massachusetts gay marriage case, the Biblical concept of marriage is summarily and arrogantly rejected by four robed anti-culture warriors in favor of the newfound sanctification of homosexual behavior.

We might as well just be blunt about what's happened. According to our renegade courts, the government is not just forbidden from endorsing the Christian religion, it must now disavow its Judeo-Christian heritage. It must bastardize itself.

Sadly, chillingly, it's all based on a lie: that the Framers [of the Constitution] intended to create an impregnable wall of separation between religion and government. But whatever the

---

2. The constitutional clause states, "Congress shall make no law respecting an establishment of religion, or prohibiting the free exercise thereof."

Framers believed, they certainly didn't intend to bastardize government from its Biblical parentage the instant it was spawned. What sense would it have made for them to build our Constitution on the solid, immovable rock of Biblical principles, then immediately uproot that foundational anchor?

The courts are making quite clear their disenchantment with this wonderful document we call our Constitution, as they dismantle it bit by bit. If the prescient John Adams was correct that our Constitution is made only for a moral and religious people, perhaps before too long it will not be suitable for us.

12
Why Gays Should Oppose Same-Sex Marriage

Judith Levine

Judith Levine is an activist for free speech and sex education and a journalist who has written about sex, gender, and families for two decades in national publications such as Ms., *the* Village Voice, *and* Harper's.

On the one hand, the legal recognition of gay marriage in the United States would give gay and lesbian couples the rights and benefits that heterosexual couples enjoy. On the other hand, legalizing gay marriage could exact a dangerous price because it would give married gays and lesbians political, cultural, and legal legitimacy while further disenfranchising those who do not fit the marriage "norm." Rather than fight for the right to marriage and its economic benefits, gay, lesbian, bisexual, and transgender people should demand tax-funded social benefits for every citizen.

First, two gay men known to their friends as "the Michaels" sealed their marriage with two rings and a champagne toast in Toronto. Then American queers broke out the bubbly when the U.S. Supreme Court declared the constitutional right to gay sex in the privacy of the bedroom, clearing the way to same-sex marriage here. If the Massachusetts Supremes rule in favor of seven same-sex couples challenging that state's marriage statute,[1] Provincetown could see a run on champagne flutes.

It's not hard to understand why America's Michaels (and Michaelas) want the right to marry. With the nuptials comes a truckload of rights of marriage, including the secure habitation of your joint home, custody of your kids, tax-free inheritance of your partner's property, and citizenship in her country. And that's not to mention the nongovernmental goodies, from health insurance to joint gym memberships to Le Creuset casseroles showered on the wedded pair along with the rice. For all that, marriage is a bargain. In New York City, licenses go for $30.

> **❝ Gay marriage won't help the leather queen. ❞**

From a civil rights standpoint, the correctness of gay marriage is obvious. To forbid the status to couples in possession of matching genitals, when the complementary-genitalia crowd is welcome at the altar, denies a class of citizens equality under the law. As long as marriage exists, the status must be open to all adults straight, [gay, lesbian, bisexual, transgender, queer,] or not sexually connected at all. A strong argument being made on behalf of the Massachusetts plaintiffs is that the current law violates the state constitution's declaration that "all people are born free and equal."

But many gay marriage advocates want more than legal freedom and equality. Understandably, they want what the state confers on their straight friends' relationships: sentimental and moral validation. Vermont's Freedom to Marry Task Force pronounced civil unions a "bitter compromise"—and not just because the law won't affect Social Security or federal taxes. To win fence-sitters' votes, the bill's authors retained all of marriage's rights but silenced its religious resonance. For instance, where a marriage is *solemnized* (the church organ swells), a [civil union] is *certified* (a bureaucrat's stamp thuds). This dispassion seemed to add insult to the substantial injury of exclu-

---

1. On November 18, 2003, three months after this article was published, the Massachusetts Supreme Court ruled that same-sex couples are legally entitled to marry under the state constitution.

sion from the privileged institution. As Beth Robinson, co-counsel to the plaintiffs in Baker,[2] put it, "Nobody writes songs about registered partnerships."

Still, in seeking to replicate marriage clause for clause and sacrament for sacrament, reformers may stall the achievement of real sexual freedom and social equality for everyone. For that, we need new songs.

Gay marriage, say proponents, subverts religion's hegemony over the institution, with its assumption of heterosexual reproductive pairing. It makes homosexuality more visible and therefore more acceptable, not just for judges or ER doctors but for the lesbian bride's formerly homophobic cousin. Because gay marriage renders queerness "normal," notes Yale legal scholar William Eskridge, it is both radical and conservative.

The problem with marriage

But marriage—forget the "gay" for a moment—is intrinsically conservative. It does not just normalize, it requires normality as the ticket in. Assimilating another "virtually normal" constituency, namely monogamous, long-term, homosexual couples, marriage pushes the queerer queers of all sexual persuasions—drag queens, club-crawlers, polyamorists, even ordinary single mothers or teenage lovers—further to the margins. "Marriage sanctifies some couples at the expense of others," wrote cultural critic Michael Warner. "It is selective legitimacy."

In Vermont, his words were borne out. Shortly after passage of the [2001 civil union] law, a coalition of liberal clergy implied that same-sex married people, like straight ones, are more godly than couples in unofficial unions: married gays, they wrote, "exemplify a moral good which cannot be represented by so-called registered partnership." And legitimacy is more than symbolic. As soon as the law passed, the University of Vermont announced it would no longer grant health benefits to gay and lesbian employees' domestic partners unless they got legally hitched. Straight domestic partners, because they had the option of marriage, never were eligible for these benefits; nor were other cohabiters.

---

2. In July 1997, three same-sex couples filed suit in Vermont seeking legal recognition of their marriages in *Baker v. State of Vermont*. As a result of the Vermont Supreme Court's favorable decision, the Vermont legislature instituted a parallel system (that granted same-sex couples all the rights, responsibilities, and benefits of marriage) called civil unions in July 2001.

Just as the Supreme Court's recognition of the "dignity" of private gay and lesbian sex won't help the street hustler or the backroom tryster from being hassled by the cops, gay marriage won't help the leather queen. It could even leave these outliers more vulnerable, as wedded homosexuals cease to identify as sexual outlaws.

In American history, religion and marriage go together like a horse and carriage. But (sorry to inform you, George W.) a modern secular state in a pluralistic democracy has no business affirming any religious version of relational morality. That said, abolishing marriage would leave undone what the state should do: ensure the individual and collective interests of people sharing homes, expenses, and children. "You can call it anything you want," remarks Brooklyn Law School professor and sex-law expert Nan Hunter. "But you have to have some mechanism by which people can easily, quickly, and cheaply designate another person for a whole list of purposes"—co-parent, co-homeowner, medical proxy, heir.

Civil partnerships

Instead of conceiving of these associations as "marriage lite," think of them as *personal partnerships* and the body of law regulating them as analogous to that for commercial partnerships. A housing co-op has different concerns than a medical practice, a mom-and-pop enterprise differs from a publicly traded corporation—and so do the statutes that limn them. The point is to limit the law to issues germane to the relationships it oversees. For instance, if kids are involved, they and their parents need legal protections, especially in the event of a split-up. Adultery, on the other hand, is not the state's affair.

Such instruments exist in other democracies. While only the Netherlands, Belgium, and Canada permit same-sex marriage, governments offer extensive nonmarital partnership rights for gay and straight citizens throughout Scandinavia, and less comprehensive ones in much of Europe, Australia, and New Zealand. Some require what is essentially a legal divorce to break up; others, like the French Pacte Civil de Solidarité (PaCS), can be ended after one partner notifies the court.

Because American marriage is inextricable from Christianity, it admits participants as Noah let animals onto the ark [in pairs]. But it doesn't have to be that way. In 1972 the National Coalition of Gay Organizations demanded the "repeal of all legislative provisions that restrict the sex or number of persons entering into a marriage unit; and the extension of legal benefits to all persons who cohabit regardless of sex or numbers." Would polygamy invite abuse of child brides, as feminists in Muslim countries and prosecutors in Mormon Utah charge? No. Group marriage could comprise any combination of genders. Guarantees of women's and children's rights and economic well-being would be more productive than outlawing multiple marriage.

> **"** *American reformers should demand what other industrialized democracies provide: tax-funded social benefits for every citizen.* **"**

The opportunity most tragically missed in the race to get gays into the marriage club is to unpack the "bundle" of rights and protections—notably health insurance—that now comes with the status and redistribute its contents to everyone. Marriage's sexual exclusion doesn't create unequal security in America. That's done by a system that loads responsibility for health care, child care, and disability support onto individual families and corporations. American reformers should demand what other industrialized democracies provide: tax-funded social benefits for every citizen. Even legal immigrant status needn't be dependent on whom you sleep with. French immigration officials consider that nation's civil-union equivalent as one of many eligibility factors—but not an automatic green light. That's unfair if married people get preferred treatment. But no intimate couple should. People form commitments to home and country through children, work, ideology, and community too.

Marriage is probably here for the duration. But new forms could clarify church-state separation, leaving the sacrament to the clergy but divesting them of civil authority. "The role of progressive activists is to insist that more real choices be available," says Eskridge. That's why New Jersey's activists are aiming to include same-sex couples under marriage law and also create an alternative domestic partnership.

Vermont's civil union, though it confers every state right of marriage, may be unequal because it is separate. But in other ways it's excitingly progressive. It is stripped of marriage's religious and sentimental history. It even lets in nonsexual pairs. As a concession to opponents claiming that queers would get "special rights" denied to "maiden aunts" and others barred from marriage by incest prohibitions, the drafters included a less extensive class of mutual rights and responsibilities for cohabiting kin, called "reciprocal benefits." Perhaps unwittingly, the clause mitigates much of marriage's sexual-regulatory function.

Nobody writes songs about registered partnerships. But a legal rhapsody of moral affirmation, lifted from an institution whose other job is to hand out opprobrium to deviants, is more like a hymn, and the state that writes it treads close to theocracy. The government must distribute its material and legal benefits equally. As for love, let the partners write their own vows.

13

Why Gays Should Support Same-Sex Marriage

Richard Goldstein

Richard Goldstein is an executive editor for the Village Voice *and recently published his book* The Attack Queers. *In 2001 the Gay and Lesbian Alliance Against Defamation named him columnist of the year.*

Democratic and progressive organizations have been reluctant to join the movement to legalize gay marriage because of internal dissent over the issue. Yet if conservatives succeed in preventing same-sex marriage, the damage done to civil rights and civil liberties will affect a wide range of people, not just gays and lesbians. The right's attempt to pass a federal amendment to ban same-sex marriage threatens all domestic partner arrangements and civil union statutes. Moreover, the precedent that would be set by such an unjust amendment would restrict judicial power to fight many instances of inequality. Reluctant progressives forget that legalizing gay marriage will benefit poor gay and lesbian families the most. By working to legalize gay marriage, activists will pave the way for legitimizing other relationships.

For some Democrats, gay marriage is the political equivalent of doggie doo. [Democratic political consultant] James Carville has identified it as one of those "icky" issues his party should shy away from. But the Republicans won't allow it. [In

September 2003], the Senate held its first hearing on the proposed constitutional amendment to ban same-sex marriage. Test cases are pending in several states. This wedge issue has been wedged, and the only question is the fundamental one when it comes to human rights: Which side are you on?

Usually progressives can be counted on to prod the Democrats, but not this time. Carville's comment has gone virtually unanswered by the left. There's been no crush of Hollywood celebs at fundraisers for this cause. The radical cadres that march against globalization and war haven't agitated for marriage rights. "There is virtually no opposition from progressive groups," says Evan Wolfson of the advocacy group Freedom to Marry. "The problem is a failure to speak out and get involved." From a movement noted for its passion about social justice, this lack of ardor demands to be addressed.

Mind you, plenty of progressives, queer and otherwise, have enlisted in this fight. NOW [National Organization for Women] has filed amicus briefs in several marriage cases. The Leadership Council for Civil Rights is circulating a letter among its members opposing the amendment. The NAACP [National Association for the Advancement of Colored People] is expected to sign on. But there is dissent in each of these organizations, and the divisions are sufficiently deep that activists have had to present two options: If you can't support same-sex marriage, surely you can see the danger in an amendment banning it. This approach has been fruitful, but the larger problem remains. "Whether it's due to a failure of progressives to connect the dots or a failure of gay groups to ask for their help," says Wolfson, "there's a curious silence."

Progressive arguments against gay marriage

Why the reticence? In part, it's because the right has attached this issue to fears about the future of the family, and some progressives are all too willing to fall for that line. In part, it's a question of style. Ever since the days of [American anarchist] Emma Goldman, marriage has been icky for radicals. Their image of gay culture as a "site of resistance" is threatened by the thought that these sexual outlaws might hew to the narrow if not the straight. Underlying these concerns is the fundamental reason why many feminists and sex radicals are cool to gay marriage. They worry about the unintended consequences.

"In seeking to replicate marriage," Judith Levine wrote recently in the *Village Voice*, "reformers may stall the achievement of real sexual freedom and social equality for everyone." Queer theorist Michael Warner regards marriage as part of a larger push toward gay normalcy, and he sees this trend as a threat to the variety that has flourished in the queer community, "with its ethical refusal of shame or implicitly shaming standards of dignity." Warner calls marriage "selective legitimacy."

> *If the right succeeds in barring gay marriage, the fallout will do much more to set back sexual freedom than any wedding vow.*

Both feminism and gay liberation have developed a potent critique of matrimony, exposing its relationship to repression and patriarchal privilege. Activists who cut their teeth on this reasoning are guided by it (and anyone headed for the altar would be well advised to check it out). But institutions change, and—thanks largely to agitation by radicals—marriage today is (or can be) different from the prison many older feminists escaped. Yet these memories of underdevelopment color the reaction of progs [progressives] like *The Nation's* Katha Pollit, whose column on gay marriage was called "Don't Say I Didn't Warn You."

"Why should straights be the only ones to have their unenforceable promise to love, honor and cherish trap them like houseflies in the web of law?" Pollit wrote. "Marriage will not only open up to gay men and lesbians whole new vistas of guilt, frustration, claustrophobia, bewilderment, declining self-esteem, unfairness, and sorrow, it will offer them the opportunity to prolong this misery by tormenting each other in court." Sage as these caveats are, they have a "Let them eat wedding cake" air. There's a difference between repudiating an entitlement and having no right to it at all. The former breeds a certain fatalism; the latter can sow the seeds of change.

Why gay marriage is a worthy cause

I want to argue that the radical critique of gay marriage is short-sighted in several respects. Even when it is correct—as in its claim that marriage is organized to bolster what Pollit calls "the socio-marital order"—it ignores the human capacity to transform an oppressive institution. As for the notion of normalcy, it simplifies the reasons why lesbians and gay men might want their relationships to carry the same legal weight as heterosexual ones. Major questions of civic equity and social prestige are on the line; this is much more than a flight from the creative anarchy of queer life. What gays are fighting for is the option to marry, not the obligation to do so—and choice, as all progressives should know, is the essence of freedom. In that sense, there's a connection between same-sex marriage and abortion rights. That's why both issues are central to the culture wars.

If the right succeeds in barring gay marriage, the fallout will do much more to set back sexual freedom than any wedding vow. The proposed amendment stipulates that no state constitution can be read in a way that extends the "incidents" of marriage to same-sex couples. In other words, all domestic-partner arrangements and civil-union statutes that come by court order will be voided. Only laws that emanate from legislatures or policies enacted by private companies would be valid. The result will be a patchwork of procedures varying so dramatically that no unmarried couple will be sure of the right to inherit assets, retain custody of children, carry a partner's health insurance, or even visit a loved one in the hospital. (It's worth noting that even in New York City the tradition of forcing lovers to identify themselves as siblings in order to be with their mates in the intensive-care unit is still alive.)

> **❝** *Same-sex marriage is a black, working-class, women's issue.* **❞**

The panic over gay unions obscures this hidden agenda, but rest assured that the real object of the right's campaign is straights who stray. The same people who are agitating for the amendment don't intend to stop there. The next thing they will go after is what they call "divorce on demand." Feminists who recoil at the thought of supporting marriage rights should consider what America will be like if everyone except homosexuals is coerced into matrimony.

And that's just the start. In weakening the role of the judiciary, this amendment would be a powerful tool in halting the advance of civil rights. All potential victims of discrimination should be aware that, for the first time ever, the Constitution would restrict the ability of judges to fight inequality. What's more, courts stacked with conservatives could strike down decisions that have nothing to do with marriage, applying the logic of this amendment just as liberal judges have used the Bill of Rights to establish many of the liberties we enjoy today. The principle so eloquently articulated by Justice Anthony Kennedy in his ruling against sodomy laws—that the Constitution allows each generation to expand the terrain of freedom—will be effectively moot once that process has been abridged.

Social class and gay marriage

What stops some lefties from applying their libertarian instincts to this issue? The most inexcusable reflex is the one that casts gay marriage as a bourgeois exercise in assimilation. It hardly helps that the loudest voices on this issue belong to gay conservatives who have framed it in similar terms. The media abet this image by selecting gay couples that can afford to travel to Canada, or that are tony enough to qualify for nuptial notices. To focus on poor people in a gay story is rare enough; but to show such folks fighting for marital benefits threatens the upbeat image the media feel compelled to project. Marriage activists aren't much more discerning. As a result, those who get to speak don't look like working stiffs.

But there are many more poor queer families than meets the media's eye, and they are the ones who stand to gain the most from marriage rights. As things are, they may not qualify for public housing; family courts may not accept their claims of domestic abuse; hospitals can—and regularly do—dismiss their right to make medical decisions on behalf of a loved one; they lack the standing to sue for a partner's wrongful death; they can't count on a partner's social security; and even when private pensions are passed along, the tax-exempt status is lost if the recipient is an unmarried mate.

Child custody, always a perilous pursuit for gay couples, is an almost Sisyphean task for the queer poor, especially in Southern or Midwestern states with laws and policies denying legal recognition to domestic partnerships. It isn't widely known that 34 percent of lesbian and gay couples in the South are raising kids. That's more than any other region, but not by much; about a third of lesbian households in America contain children. (Among gay men, it's a fifth.) Census data also suggest that lesbians of color are more likely than white dykes to have kids at home. In other words, same-sex marriage is a black, working-class, women's issue, despite its palmy facade.

But doesn't this argue for a system in which benefits aren't tied to marriage at all? "Even as we support legalizing same-sex unions," Pollit writes, "we might ask whether we want to distribute these rights and privileges according to marital status. Why should access to health care be a by-product of a legalized sexual connection, gay or straight?" Wouldn't we all be better off if everyone raising a child were entitled to the same break? And why not allow people to structure their intimate lives as they choose without sacrificing security? Generations of radicals have imagined a world in which the norm-making rules of matrimony are suspended—or at least loosened to suit the way people actually live. This is a struggle worth waging. Why do radicals assume it will be hindered if gay people can wed?

> *The growing range of options both within and outside marriage is a reality not just in America but across the West.*

It's understandable that advocates for gay marriage would portray it as a tribute to normalcy, and in the short term it probably will look like that. But as gay people grow accustomed to this option they will shape it to suit their particular needs. You'll see leather weddings, boi-on-boi [boy-on-boy] unions between queers of the opposite sex, trans matches that defy the boundaries of gender—all in cahoots with rice-throwing, trip-to-Niagara realness. Queers won't stop being queer just because they can get hitched. The tradition of open relationships won't cease to exist, nor will the boundless exploration of identity and desire. Marriage won't change gay people, but merely affirm them as they are—and that, in all its profane glory, isn't so different from what straight people have become.

The vogue for white weddings notwithstanding, most young heterosexuals entering the state of matrimony have very different expectations than their parents did. Some take their vows as a statement of eternal fidelity, others regard them as the affirmation of a loving but not necessarily lifelong bond;

some are laying the groundwork for having children, while others are focused on fitting their kids from prior unions into a new whole. For each of these strategies, there are couples that mean to accomplish the same goals without hitching up. The growing range of options both within and outside marriage is a reality not just in America but across the West, and the law is evolving accordingly. The right's anxiety about gay unions has everything to do with this new flexibility. The more patterns of intimacy change, the more conservatives rush to keep the form of marriage the same.

It's debatable whether allowing gay people to wed will open the floodgates to recognition for other relationships. But certainly civil unions present a model that can be broadly applied. I'm not thinking of [Republican senator] Rick Santorum's specter of incest and polygamy, but of the elderly who live together and don't want to sully the memory of their deceased spouses with another formal marriage. Civil unions might suit them, along with siblings who want to commemorate their bond (and join their assets). Down the road we may see groups of people sharing the custody of children, or geriatric communes seeking a legal tie. Each of these contingencies will involve its own process of agitation, and it will be up to society to accept or reject each claim. But the result could be a menu of possibilities, ranging from trial unions to so-called covenant marriages that are very difficult to leave. People may elect to pass from one category to another as their attitudes change. This begins to look like the kind of world radicals want to see—a world of choice.

Gay marriage won't bring that about; nor will banning gay marriage prevent it. But the outcome of this struggle could determine whether America will adhere to a rigid code of intimacy, enforced by a system of penalties and stigma, or evolve toward the democratic vistas our poets have foreseen. "The greatest lessons of Nature," wrote [poet] Walt Whitman, are "the lessons of variety and freedom." America, he believed, was the ultimate repository of that principle. If we see gay marriage in that light—as an emblem of variety and freedom manifest in love—we can understand why the right feels compelled to crush it. And we can see why the left must defend it, if only for its potential as a radical act.

14

The Gay Marriage Debate Exposes Heterosexual Hypocrisy

Froma Harrop

Froma Harrop's twice-weekly syndicated column appears in numerous newspapers across the United States. She is also on the editorial board for the Rhode Island Providence Journal.

Conservatives who oppose gay marriage often present two main arguments: 1) preserving a traditional legal definition of marriage ensures that children will live in homes with dedicated mothers and fathers, and 2) gay marriage threatens the ethos of monogamy. However, heterosexual marriages are increasingly failing to provide children with the ideal stable home life. In truth, only about half of American children live with their original married parents. Moreover, some studies show that heterosexual married men are no more monogamous than gay men in committed relationships. Heterosexuals who demonstrate little regard for the sanctity of their own marriages are to blame for undermining family life in the United States, not gay and lesbian couples seeking equality in marriage.

Social conservatives battling gay marriage would have an easier time of it were it not for one thing: the sorry example of heterosexual marriages. Better to obsess over proposals to extend legal recognition to same-sex unions. That affords a fine opportunity to avoid addressing the real threat to American children, which is the instability of their parents' relationship.

Maggie Gallagher argues in *The Weekly Standard* that gay men and lesbian women cannot possibly participate in the institution designed so that "children have loving, committed mothers and fathers." Allowing gay marriage, she writes, "would require society to gut marriage of its central presumptions about family in order to accommodate a few adults' desires."

Heterosexuals should look in the mirror

If Gallagher wants to make a case that the ideal set-up for children is to live in a household headed by their married mother and father, I'm in her camp. But the "adult desires" detrimental to that happy situation are chiefly heterosexual. The mating habits of the homosexual minority have little to do with the vast sea of heartbreak and insecurity confronting American children today.

Put bluntly, the foray into hand-wringing over gay unions is an exercise in scapegoating and evasion. And the reason for it is obvious: Most social conservatives don't want to offend an American mainstream that's been going downhill. Too many votes.

Today, only about half of American children live with their original set of married parents. The rest stay with single parents, or non-relatives, or parents who never married, or biological parents and their new spouse. This is the reality. While many of these parental figures work hard at doing the right thing, their relationships do not meet Gallagher's gold standard for parenthood.

> *The image that makes me think of polygamy isn't a gay couple but Newt Gingrich and his three wives.*

Conservatives who argue that marriage is all about children should get a lot pickier about which heterosexual pairings qualify. More than half of all married couples, about 54 percent, do not have children under the age of 18. Yet, no social conservative I know of suggests that these couples be denied the tax breaks and legal protections available to married people. What's so special about being in a childless third marriage?

Also writing in *The Weekly Standard*, Stanley Kurtz makes the silly argument that recognizing gay marriages puts us on a slippery slope to approving polygamy. "The trouble is," he writes, "gay marriage itself threatens the ethos of monogamy."

As evidence, Kurtz points to a study showing that 20 percent of gay males who had participated in a "commitment ceremony" did not practice monogamy. It took a certain amount of guts to use that number to support his argument. A University of San Francisco study found that 24 percent of married heterosexual men have had sex with partners other than their wives.

Kurtz makes the logically desperate claim that because certain libertarians back both the legalization of gay marriage and polygamy, one inevitably leads to the other. That's like saying the following: Froma Harrop thinks drunken driving and SUVs are both dangers on the road. Therefore, criminalizing drunken driving will lead to a ban on SUVs. (If only!)

The slippery slope here is serial monogamy. The image that makes me think of polygamy isn't a gay couple but Newt Gingrich and his three wives. Despite his blatant disregard for the vows of marriage, social conservatives still sit at the former House speaker's knee for lectures on saving American civilization. Gingrich now serves as a Distinguished Visiting Fellow at the Hoover Institution, the conservative think tank (which employs Kurtz).

If the public doesn't take the traditional definitions of marriage as seriously as it once did, the reason is not permissive liberalism but sloppy conservatism. With some admirable exceptions, conservatives have long skated around the marital chaos spreading right under their noses.

That the Bible Belt is home to some of the highest divorce rates in the country should give these people pause. When will they speak uncomfortable truths to self-described conservatives who put their own "adult desires" above their children's welfare?

One doesn't have to be a conservative to express grave concern over the increasingly fractured home life of American children. Given the magnitude of this crisis, focusing on gay marriage as a knife pointed at the social fabric seems an exercise in absurdity.

Organizations to Contact

The editors have compiled the following list of organizations concerned with the issues debated in this book. The descriptions are derived from materials provided by the organizations. All have publications or information available for interested readers. The list was compiled on the date of publication of the present volume; names, addresses, phone and fax numbers, and e-mail and Web site addresses may change. Be aware that many organizations take several weeks or longer to respond to inquiries, so allow as much time as possible.

Abiding Truth Ministries
5150 Sunrise Ave., Suite H-4, Fair Oaks, CA 95628
(916) 965-8925
e-mail: info@abidingtruth.com • Web site: www.abidingtruth.com

Abiding Truth Ministries provides resources and funding for conservative Christian activists to promote traditional family values in their communities. The organization's Pro-Family Law Center and Rescue the Schools Campaign fight against same-sex marriage and gay and lesbian political power. Abiding Truth publishes numerous books, position papers, and pamphlets, including "A Christian Defense of the Natural Family" and "'Gay Marriage' Violates the 'Law Above the Law.'"

Alliance Defense Fund (ADF)
15333 North Pima Rd., Suite 165, Scottsdale, AZ 85260
(800) 835-5233 • fax: (480) 444-0025
e-mail: info@telladf.org • Web site: www.alliancedefensefund.org

ADF provides funding, legal support, and training to organizations that support conservative Christian values, religious freedom, and the traditional family in the United States. It trains church and civic leaders to fight against same-sex marriage, legalized abortion, and assisted suicide. ADF conducts the National Litigation Academy to educate attorneys and provide pro bono legal assistance in national and local cases.

Alliance for Marriage (AFM)
PO Box 2490, Merrifield, VA 22116
(703) 934-1212 • fax: (703) 934-1211
e-mail: info@allianceformarriage.org
Web site: www.allianceformarriage.org

The Alliance for Marriage is a nonprofit organization dedicated to promoting traditional marriage and addressing fatherless families in the United States. AFM works to prevent gay marriage and to educate the public, the media, elected officials, and civil leaders on the benefits of heterosexual marriage for children, adults, and society.

American Civil Liberties Union (ACLU), Lesbian and Gay Rights Project
125 Broad St., 18th Fl., New York, NY 10004
(212) 549-2627
Web site: www.aclu.org/LesbianGayRights/LesbianGayRightsmain.cfm

The ACLU is the nation's oldest and largest civil liberties organization. Its Lesbian and Gay Rights Project, started in 1986, handles litigation, education, and public policy work on behalf of gays and lesbians. The union supports same-sex marriage. It publishes the monthly newsletter *Civil Liberties Alert*, the handbook *The Rights of Lesbians and Gay Men*, the briefing paper "Lesbian and Gay Rights," and the books *The Rights of Families: The ACLU Guide to the Rights of Today's Family Members* and *Making Schools Safe: An Anti-Harassment Training Program for Schools*.

American Family Association (AFA)
PO Drawer 2440, Tupelo, MS 38803
(662) 844-5036 • fax: (662) 842-7798
Web site: www.afa.net

The AFA works to promote traditional family values in the media and entertainment industries by motivating and equipping citizens to change the culture to reflect biblical ideals. Opposed to gay marriage, the organization lobbies elected officials and media venues to resist what it calls "the homosexual agenda." The AFA publishes numerous position papers, the monthly *AFA Journal*, and the newsletter *AFA Action Alert*.

Canadian Lesbian and Gay Archives
PO Box 639, Station A, Toronto, ON M5W 1G2 Canada
(416) 777-2755
e-mail: queeries@clga.ca • Web site: www.clga.ca

The archives collects and maintains information and materials relating to the gay and lesbian rights movement in Canada and elsewhere. Its collection of records and other materials documenting the stories of lesbians and gay men and their organizations in Canada is available to the public for the purpose of education and research. It has published numerous books and pamphlets and publishes an annual newsletter, *Lesbian and Gay Archivist*.

Children of Lesbians and Gay Everywhere (COLAGE)
3543 Eighteenth St. #1, San Francisco, CA 94110
(415) 861-KIDS (5437) • fax: (415) 255-8345
e-mail: colage@colage.org • Web site: www.colage.org

COLAGE is an international organization to support young people with gay, lesbian, bisexual, or transgendered parents. It coordinates pen pal and scholarship programs and sponsors an annual Family Week to celebrate family diversity. COLAGE publishes a quarterly newsletter and maintains several e-mail discussion lists.

Christian Coalition of America (CC)
PO Box 37030, Washington, DC 20013
(202) 479-6900 • fax: (202) 479-4260
e-mail: coalition@cc.org • Web site: www.cc.org

The Christian Coalition of America is one of the largest Christian grassroots organizations in the United States. The organization helps conservative Christians to become active in their local, state, and national government through voter education, lobbying Congress and the White House, and training organizers around the country. The CC publishes the weekly newsletter *Washington Weekly Review*.

Citizens for Community Values (CCV)
11175 Reading Rd., Suite 103, Cincinnati, OH 45241
(513) 733-5775 • fax: (513) 733-5794
e-mail: info@ccv.org • Web site: www.ccv.org

Citizens for Community Values exists to promote Judeo-Christian moral values and to reduce destructive behaviors contrary to those values through education, active community partnership, and individual empowerment at the local, state, and national levels. The CCV believes that gay and lesbian rights activism presents one of the greatest threats to traditional family values. It operates a speakers bureau and publishes the quarterly newsletter *Citizens' Courier*.

Concerned Women for America (CWA)
1015 Fifteenth St. NW, Suite 1100, Washington, DC 20005
(202) 488-7000 • fax: (202) 488-0806
Web site: www.cwfa.org

The CWA is an educational and legal defense foundation that seeks to strengthen the traditional family by applying Judeo-Christian moral standards. It opposes gay marriage and the granting of additional civil rights protections to gays and lesbians. It publishes the monthly magazine *Family Voice* and various position papers on gay marriage and other issues.

Eagle Forum
PO Box 618, Alton, IL 62002
(618) 462-5415 • fax: (618) 462-8909
e-mail: eagle@eagleforum.org • Web site: www.eagleforum.org

A political action group, Eagle Forum advocates traditional biblical values. It believes mothers should stay home with their children, and it favors policies that support the traditional family and reduce government involvement in family issues. The forum opposes an equal rights amendment and gay rights legislation. It publishes the monthly *Phyllis Schlafly Report* and *Education Reporter*.

Equal Marriage for Same-Sex Couples
c/o Kevin Bourassa and Joe Varnell, Bruce E. Walker Law Office
65 Wellesley St. East, Suite 205, Toronto, ON M4Y 1G7 Canada
(416) 961-7451
e-mail: samesex@samesexmarriage.ca • Web site: www.samesexmarriage.ca

Equal Marriage was started in 2001 by Kevin Bourassa and Joe Varnell when their Toronto Metropolitan Community Church went to court (with several same-sex couples) in Ontario, Canada, seeking government recognition of civil gay marriage. The organization acts as a clearinghouse of legal information about same-sex marriage in Canada and the United States, a center for legal and social action, and publishes an e-mail newsletter.

Family Pride Coalition
PO Box 65327, Washington, DC 20035
(202) 331-5015 • fax: (202) 331-0080
e-mail: info@familypride.org • Web site: www.familypride.org

The coalition advocates for the well-being of lesbian, gay, bisexual, and trans-gendered (LGBT) parents and their families through mutual support, community collaboration, and public understanding. It lobbies for positive public policy, educates communities about LGBT families, and provides information for LGBT families to enhance their lives. Family Pride publishes numerous pamphlets such as *How to Talk to Children About Our Families* and the quarterly newsletter *Family Tree.*

Family Research Council (FRC)
801 G St. NW, Washington, DC 20001
(202) 393-2100 • fax: (202) 393-2134
Web site: www.frc.org

The council is a research and educational organization that promotes the traditional family, which the council defines as a group of people bound by marriage, blood, or adoption. The council opposes gay marriage and adoption rights. It publishes numerous reports from a conservative perspective on issues affecting the family, including "Free to Be Family." Among its other publications are the monthly newsletters *State of the Family, Washington Watch,* and the semiannual journal *Family Policy Review.*

Family Research Institute (FRI)
PO Box 62640, Colorado Springs, CO 80962
(303) 681-3113
Web site: www.familyresearchinst.org

The FRI distributes information about family, sexual, and substance abuse issues. The institute believes that strengthening traditional marriage would reduce many social problems, including crime, poverty, and sexually transmitted diseases. The FRI publishes the monthly newsletter *Family Research Report* as well as the pamphlets *Same-Sex Marriage: Til Death Do Us Part??* and *Homosexual Parents: A Comparative Study.*

Focus on the Family
8685 Explorer Dr., Colorado Springs, CO 80920
(719) 531-3400 • (800) 232-6459
Web site: www.family.org

Focus on the Family is a Christian organization that seeks to strengthen the traditional family in America and opposes gay marriage. It believes the family is the most important social unit and maintains that reestablishing the traditional two-parent family will end many social problems. In addition to conducting research and educational programs, Focus on the Family publishes the monthly periodicals *Focus on the Family* and *Citizen* as well as the reports *Setting the Record Straight: What Research Really Says About the Consequences of Homosexuality* and *Twice as Strong: The Undeniable Advantages of Raising Children in a Traditional Two-Parent Family.*

The Howard Center for Family, Religion, and Society
934 N. Main St., Rockford, IL 61103
(815) 964-5819 • fax: (815) 965-1826
Web site: www.profam.org

The Howard Center conducts research to affirm the traditional family and religion as the foundation of a virtuous society. The organization operates the John L. Swan Library on Family and Culture, a large collection of conservative family literature. The center publishes the monthly periodicals *Family in America* and *Religion & Society Report* and the supplemental *New Research* newsletter.

Human Rights Campaign FamilyNet (HRC FamilyNet)
1640 Rhode Island Ave. NW, Washington, DC 20036
(202) 628-4160 • (800) 777-4723
e-mail: hrc@hrc.org
Web site: www.hrc.org/Template.cfm?Section=About_HRC_FamilyNet

HRC FamilyNet is a clearinghouse of information for lesbian, gay, bisexual, and transgendered families coordinated by the Human Rights Campaign Foundation. It provides information and resources about adoption, gay marriage, civil unions, coming out, custody and visitation, donor insemination, family law, families of origin, marriage, money, parenting, religion, schools, senior health and housing, state laws and legislation, straight spouses, and transgender and workplace issues. FamilyNet publishes numerous reports and the biweekly *HRC FamilyNet News*.

IntiNet Resource Center
PO Box 4322-C, San Rafael, CA 94913
e-mail: pad@well.sf.ca.com

The center promotes nonmonogamous relationships as an alternative to the traditional family. It also serves as a clearinghouse for information on nonmonogamous relationships and as a network for people interested in alternative family lifestyles. IntiNet publishes the quarterly newsletter *Floodtide*, the book *Polyamory: The New Love Without Limits*, and the *Resource Guide for the Responsible Non-Monogamist*.

Lambda Legal Defense and Education Fund
120 Wall St., Suite 1500, New York, NY 10005
(212) 809-8585 • fax: (212) 809-0055
Web site: www.lambdalegal.org

Lambda is a public interest law firm committed to achieving full recognition of the civil rights of lesbians, gay men, and people with HIV/AIDS. The firm addresses a variety of topics, including equal marriage rights, parenting and relationship issues, and domestic partner benefits. It believes marriage is a basic right and an individual choice. Lambda publishes the quarterly *Lambda Update*, the pamphlet *Freedom to Marry*, and several position papers on same-sex marriage and gay and lesbian family rights.

Loving More
PO Box 4358, Boulder, CO 80306
(303) 534-7540 • (800) 424-9561
e-mail: marywolf@lovemore.com • Web site: www.lovemore.com

Loving More explores and supports many different forms of family and relationships. It promotes alternative relationship options—such as open marriage, extended family, and multipartner marriages—and serves as a national clearinghouse for the multipartner movement. The organization publishes the quarterly magazine *Loving More*.

MarriageWatch
Columbus School of Law
Catholic University of America, Washington, DC 20064
(202) 319-6215
e-mail: info@marriagewatch.org • Web site: www.marriagewatch.org

MarriageWatch is a service of the Marriage Law Project, a legal research project established to reaffirm the legal definition of marriage as the union of one man and one woman through scholarly, legal, and educational work. Marriage-Watch offers current news related to marriage law, summaries of state marriage laws, and other resources to assist those working to protect traditional marriage. It publishes *MarriageWatch Update*, a weekly e-mail newsletter.

National Center for Lesbian Rights (NCLR)
870 Market St., Suite 370, San Francisco, CA 94102
(415) 392-8442 • fax: (415) 392-8442
e-mail: info@nclrights.org • Web site: www.nclrights.org

The center is a public interest law office that provides legal counseling and representation to victims of sexual orientation discrimination. Primary areas of advice include child custody and parenting, employment, housing, the military, and insurance. Among the center's publications are the pamphlets *Same-Sex Relationship Recognition* and *Adoption by Lesbian, Gay, Bisexual, and Transgender Parents: An Overview of the Current Law.*

National Gay and Lesbian Task Force (NGLTF)
1325 Massachusetts Ave. NW, Suite 600, Washington, DC 20005
(202) 393-5177 • fax: (202) 393-2241
Web site: www.ngltf.org

The NGLTF is a civil rights advocacy organization that lobbies Congress and the White House on a range of civil rights and AIDS issues affecting gays and lesbians. The organization is working to make same-sex marriage legal. It publishes numerous papers and pamphlets, the booklets *Family Policy: Issues Affecting Gay, Lesbian, Bisexual and Transgender Families* and *Massachusetts Equal Marriage Rights Policy Brief*, and the quarterly *Task Force Report.*

Parents, Families, and Friends of Lesbians and Gays (P-FLAG)
1726 M St. NW, Suite 400, Washington, DC 20036
(202) 467-8180 • fax: (202) 467-8194
Web site: www.pflag.org

P-FLAG is a national organization that provides support and education services for gays, lesbians, bisexuals, and their families and friends. It also works to end prejudice and discrimination against homosexuals. It publishes and distributes pamphlets and articles, including *Faith in Our Families, Our Daughters and Sons: Questions and Answers for Parents of Gay, Lesbian, Bisexual, and Transgendered People*, and *Hate Crimes Hurt Families.*

Religious Coalition for the Freedom to Marry (RCFM)
325 Huntington Ave., Suite 88, Boston, MA 02115-4401
(617) 848-9900
e-mail: info@rcfm.org • Web site: www.rcfm.org

The coalition supports civil marriage rights for same-gender couples and seeks to promote dialogue within faith communities about religious marriage for gay and lesbian couples. Active members include clergy from Baptist, Buddhist, Mormon, Disciples of Christ, Episcopalian, Jewish, Lutheran, Metropolitan Community Church, Presbyterian, Quaker, Unitarian Universalist, United Church of Christ, and other religious organizations. RCFM educates communities, lobbies legislatures, and circulates for signatures the "Massachusetts Declaration of Religious Support for the Freedom of Same-Sex Couples to Marry."

Traditional Values Coalition (TVC)
139 C St. SE, Washington, DC 20003
(202) 547-8570 • fax: (202) 546-6403
Web site: www.traditionalvalues.org

The coalition strives to restore what the group believes are the traditional moral and spiritual values in American government, schools, media, and society. It believes that gay marriage threatens the family unit and extends civil rights beyond what the coalition considers appropriate limits. The coalition publishes the newsletter *TVC Weekly News* as well as various information papers addressing same-sex marriage and other issues.

Unitarian Universalist Association (UUA)
Office of Bisexual, Gay, Lesbian and Transgender Concerns
25 Beacon St., Boston, MA 02108
(617) 742-2100
Web site: www.uua.org/obgltc

The Unitarian Universalist Association is a liberal religious organization that has actively supported equal rights for lesbian, gay, bisexual, and transgender people since 1961. Many ministers in UUA churches conduct holy union ceremonies for LGBT couples. Over 411 congregations have become "Welcoming Congregations" that specifically support LGBT rights and provide a welcoming atmosphere for LGBT members and visitors. The Office of Bisexual, Gay, Lesbian and Transgender Concerns provides resources, instructional courses, and helps congregations to fight against discrimination. The UUA publishes the monthly magazine *UUWorld*.

Universal Fellowship of Metropolitan Community Churches (UFMCC)
8704 Santa Monica Blvd., 2nd Floor, West Hollywood, CA 90069
(310) 360-8640 • fax: (310) 360-8680
Web site: www.mccchurch.org

The UFMCC supports the lesbian and gay community with three hundred churches in eighteen countries. It publishes a wide range of materials on topics concerning religion and homosexuality, including *Not a Sin, Not a Sickness* and *The Lord Is My Shepherd & He Knows I'm Gay*.

Bibliography

Books

Jack O. Balswick and Judith K. Balswick — *The Family: A Christian Perspective on the Contemporary Home*. Grand Rapids, MI: Baker Book House, 1999.

Nijole V. Benokraitus — *Feuds About Families: Conservative, Centrist, Liberal, and Feminist Perspectives*. New York: Prentice-Hall, 1999.

Robert A. Bernstein, Betty DeGeneres, and Robert MacNeil — *Straight Parents, Gay Children: Keeping Families Together*. New York: Thunder's Mouth, 2003.

Stephanie A. Brill — *The Queer Parent's Primer: A Lesbian and Gay Families' Guide to Navigating Through a Straight World*. Oakland, CA: New Harbinger, 2001.

Christopher Carrington — *No Place Like Home: Relationships and Family Life Among Lesbians and Gay Men*. Chicago: University of Chicago Press, 1999.

D. Merilee Clunis and G. Dorsey Green — *The Lesbian Parenting Book: A Guide to Creating Families and Raising Children*. Seattle: Seal, 2003.

Hayden Curry, Frederick Hertz, and Denis Clifford — *A Legal Guide for Lesbian and Gay Couples*. Berkeley, CA: NOLO, 2004.

Martin Dupius — *Same-Sex Marriage, Legal Mobilization, and the Politics of Rights*. New York: Peter Lang, 2002.

Marvin Mahan Ellison — *Same-Sex Marriage?: A Christian Ethical Analysis*. Cleveland, OH: Pilgrim, 2004.

William N. Eskridge and William N. Eskridge Jr. — *Equality Practice: Civil Unions and the Future of Gay Rights*. New York: Routledge, 2001.

Elizabeth Freeman — *The Wedding Complex: Forms of Belonging in Modern American Culture*. Durham, NC: Duke University Press, 2002.

Abigail Garner — *Families Like Mine: Children of Gay Parents Tell It Like It Is*. New York: HarperCollins, 2004.

Evan Gerstmann — *Same-Sex Marriage and the Constitution*. New York: Cambridge University Press, 2003.

Richard Goldstein — *The Attack Queers: Liberal Society and the Gay Right*. New York: Verso, 2002.

Andrew R. Gottlieb — *Out of the Twilight: Fathers of Gay Men Speak*. New York: Haworth, 2000.

Andrew R. Gottlieb	*Sons Talk About Their Gay Fathers: Life's Curves.* New York: Harrington Park, 2003.
Lynn Haley-Banez and Joanne Garrett	*Lesbians in Committed Relationships: Extraordinary Couples, Ordinary Lives.* New York: Harrington Park, 2002.
Hendrik Hartog	*Man and Wife in America: A History.* Cambridge, MA: Harvard University Press, 2002.
Daniel A. Helminiak	*What the Bible Really Says About Homosexuality.* San Francisco: Alamo Square, 2000.
Anne Hendershott and Jorge Masetti	*The Politics of Deviance.* San Francisco: Encounter, 2004.
Janet R. Jakobsen and Ann Pellegrini	*Love the Sin: Sexual Regulation and the Limits of Tolerance.* Boston: Beacon, 2004.
Robert Lewis and Stu Weber	*Raising a Modern-Day Knight: A Father's Role in Guiding His Son to Authentic Manhood.* Colorado Springs, CO: Focus on the Family, 1999.
Stephen Macedo and Iris Marion Young	*Child, Family, and State.* New York: New York University Press, 2003.
Gerald P. Mallon	*Gay Men Choosing Parenthood.* New York: Columbia University Press, 2004.
Michael Mello	*Legalizing Gay Marriage: Vermont and the National Debate.* Philadelphia: Temple University Press, 2004.
David Moats	*Civil Wars: Gay Marriage in America.* New York: Harcourt, 2004.
Joseph Nicolosi and Linda Ames Nicolosi	*A Parent's Guide to Preventing Homosexuality.* Downers Grove, IL: InterVarsity, 2002.
Jonathan Rauch	*Gay Marriage: Why It Is Good for Gays, Good for Straights, and Good for America.* New York: Times, 2004.
Alan Sears and Craig Osten	*The Homosexual Agenda: Exposing the Principal Threat to Religious Freedom Today.* Nashville: Broadman and Holman, 2003.
Ralph R. Smith and Russel R. Windes	*Progay/Antigay: The Rhetorical War over Sexuality.* Thousand Oaks, CA: Sage, 2000.
Judith E. Snow	*How It Feels to Have a Lesbian or Gay Parent: A Book by Kids for Kids of All Ages.* New York: Harrington Park, 2004.
Gretchen A. Stiers	*From This Day Forward: Commitment, Marriage, and Family in Lesbian and Gay Relationships.* New York: Palgrave Macmillan, 2000.
John R.W. Stott	*Same-Sex Partnerships? A Christian Perspective.* New York: Fleming H. Revell, 1998.
David Strah and Susanna Margolis	*Gay Dads: A Celebration of Fatherhood.* Los Angeles: J.P. Tarcher, 2003.

Mark Strasser	*On Same-Sex Marriage, Civil Unions, and the Rule of Law: Constitutional Interpretation at the Crossroads.* New York: Praeger, 2002.
Linda Waite and Maggie Gallagher	*The Case for Marriage: Why Married People Are Happier, Healthier, and Better Off Financially.* Louisville, KY: Broadway, 2001.
Lynn D. Wardle et al.	*Marriage and Same-Sex Unions: A Debate.* New York: Praeger, 2003.
Jeffrey Weeks, Brian Heaphy, and Catherine Donovan	*Same-Sex Intimacies: Families of Choice and Other Life Experiments.* New York: Routledge, 2001.
Bonnie Zimmerman	*Lesbian Histories and Cultures: An Encyclopedia.* New York: Garland, 2000.

Periodicals

Advocate	"Candidates for Marriage," February 3, 2004.
Advocate	"Our Readers Get Married," February 17, 2004.
Joshua K. Baker	"Summary of Opinion Research on Same-Sex Marriage," *iMAPP Policy Brief*, December 5, 2003.
Karen Breslau et al.	"Outlaw Vows," *Newsweek*, March 1, 2004.
Chris Bull	"What Makes a Mom," *Advocate*, November 25, 2003.
Christianity Today	"Let No Law Put Asunder," February 2004.
Rachel Clarke	"Gay Marriage Ruling 'Threatens U.S. Soul,'" *BBC News*, November 18, 2003.
Victoria Clarke	"What About the Children? Arguments Against Lesbian and Gay Parenting," *Women's Studies International Forum*, September/October 2001.
Lynette Clemetson	"Both Sides Court Black Churches in the Battle over Gay Marriage," *New York Times*, March 1, 2004.
Alan Cooperman	"Episcopal Vote Allows Blessings of Gay Unions," *Washington Post*, August 7, 2003.
CQ Researcher	"Disputed Studies Give Gay Parents Good Marks," September 5, 2003.
Lisa Duggan	"Holy Matrimony!" *Nation*, March 15, 2004.
Economist	"Out in Front," February 21, 2004.
Franklin Foer	"Marriage Counselor," *Atlantic Monthly*, March 2004.
Dan Gilgoff et al.	"Tied in Knots by Gay Marriage," *U.S. News & World Report*, March 8, 2004.
Richard Goldstein	"It's the Symbolism, Stupid: Gay Marriage and the Future of American Politics," *Village Voice*, February 11–17, 2004.
Erica Goode	"A Rainbow of Differences in Gays' Children," *New York Times*, July 17, 2001.

John W. Kennedy   "Gay Parenting on Trial," *Christianity Today*, July 8, 2002.

Stanley Kurtz   "Oh Canada! Will Gay Marriage Stand?" *National Review*, June 13, 2003.

Richard Lacayo   "For Better or for Worse?" *Time*, February 29, 2004.

Joseph Landau   "Misjudged: What *Lawrence* Hasn't Wrought," *New Republic*, February 16, 2004.

Carolyn Lochhead   "Gay Marriage Momentum Stuns Both Backers and Foes," *San Francisco Chronicle*, March 5, 2004.

Rona Marech   "Devastating Side of Gay Liberation: Straight Spouse Network Eases Pain," *San Francisco Chronicle*, January 6, 2003.

Michael McAuliffe   "Love and the Law," *National*, May 19, 1999.

National Review   "The Right Amendment," January 26, 2004.

George Neumayr   "Marriage on the Rocks," *American Spectator*, February 2004.

Newsweek   "The War over Gay Marriage," July 7, 2003.

New York Times   "Putting Bias in the Constitution," February 25, 2004.

Dennis O'Brien   "A More Perfect Union," *Christian Century*, January 27, 2004.

John O'Sullivan   "The Bells Are Ringing . . . ," *National Review*, March 8, 2004.

Karen Peterson   "Gay Marriage a Complex Political, Legal Issue," *Stateline.org*, 2003.

Katha Pollitt   "Adam and Steve: Together at Last," *Nation*, December 15, 2003.

Katha Pollitt   "Polymaritally Perverse," *Nation*, October 4, 1999.

Jim Rinnert   "The Trouble with Gay Marriage," *In These Times*, December 30, 2003.

Reggie Rivers   "Same-Sex Marriage an Eventuality," *Denver Post*, November 21, 2003.

Robert Scheer   "Bush Plays Pope on Gay Marriage," *Nation*, August 18, 2003.

Bob Schwartz   "In Defense of Gay Marriage," *In These Times*, February 6, 2004.

Leslie Scrivener   "Toronto Priest Backs Same-Sex Marriage," *Toronto Star*, February 5, 2004.

Scott Sherman   "Our Son Is Happy, What Else Matters?" *Newsweek*, September 16, 2002.

Thomas Sowell   "Gay Marriage Issue Is Really About Keeping the Rule of Law," *Salt Lake Tribune*, March 5, 2004.

Andrew Sullivan   "Why the M Word Matters to Me," *Time*, February 16, 2004.

Michelle Tauber   "Sweet Harmony," *People*, February 23, 2004.
and Julie Jordan

Chris Taylor   "I Do . . . No You Don't!" *Time*, March 1, 2004.

Jyoti Thottam   "Why Breaking Up Is So Hard to Do," *Time*, March 1, 2004.

USA Today Magazine   "Adoption More Open for Gays and Lesbians," April 2003.

David Usborne   "Gay with Children," *New York*, November 3, 2003.

Jacqueline Woodson   "Motherhood, My Way," *Essence*, December 2003.

Internet Source

Glenn T. Stanton   "The Human Case Against Same-Sex Marriage," *Citizen-Link*, Focus on the Family, December 27, 2003. www.family.org/cforum/fosi/marriage/ssuap/a0029575.cfm.

Index